# HYPOCHONDRIA

## Overcoming Common Problems

# Overcoming Common Problems

## EDITOR'S PREFACE

KENYON

Overcoming Common Problems

# HYPOCHONDRIA

## Dr F. E. Kenyon
M.D., F.R.C.P. (Ed.), F.R.C.Psych.

SHELDON PRESS
LONDON

First published in Great Britain in 1978 by
Sheldon Press, Marylebone Road, London NW1 4DU

Printed in Great Britain by
Richard Clay (The Chaucer Press) Ltd, Bungay, Suffolk

ISBN 0 85969 160 8

# Contents

For J.

# Introduction

The purpose of this book is to make clear to you what hypochondria is all about. I hope it will also help you to understand yourself a little better, both your body and mind, and how they may affect each other in sickness and in health. In the process I shall show you what hypochondriacs have in common as well as how they differ. Also what sort of people tend to get this label attached to them by both doctors and others and why. Are, in fact, the same people being talked about or do doctors and laymen mean quite different things when they call somebody a hypochondriac?

How the name has been both used and misused will also be described as well as how various ideas about hypochondria fit into modern psychiatric thinking. We will meet several different types of hypochondriac, see in what particular ways they can suffer, and what can be done about it. Finally I intend to show that it is no laughing matter, as much suffering and misunderstanding can result. In some cases expert help will be required.

There are obvious pitfalls in trying to diagnose and treat yourself and I am well aware of these. Throughout this book I have tried to achieve a sensible balance as, on the one hand I don't want to put you off visiting your doctor and on the other I don't want you going unnecessarily or too often. I have at the same time suggested ways in which you might help yourself or where you can get further advice, information or help without bothering your doctor. However, if still in doubt and for your own peace of mind, do go and see your doctor.

But I think you will agree that understanding more about your condition, the fact that there is a lot known about it and that there are many other fellow sufferers, all helps to make it less frightening and more bearable. As you will soon find out, in many ways we are all potential hypochondriacs and certainly many of us pass through phases of being one and so know what it's like from personal experience.

# I

## So you think you're a hypochondriac?

A hypochondriac is a person who shows a morbid pre-occupation with his body or state of health, either mental or physical, and makes this the subject of complaints to others. It is probably better to talk about hypochondriacal people, symptoms and the like; that is, to use the word as an adjective. This is because it is doubtful if there is a separate disease called hypochondria, it is rather that hypochondriacs are a mixed group with various other things wrong with them.

In any case, it is often a matter of degree or fine judgement to say when a normal concern over your body, appearance or health has turned into a morbid one. But, as already noted, there are different types of hypochondriac, some more serious than others.

In order to understand why ideas on the subject are so muddled it is necessary to think for a moment about the origin of the name itself. Like many other medical terms it has an ancient origin, which over the years has undergone several changes, ending up with both popular and technical meanings.

Hypochondria (simply putting -iasis on the end means a process or the resulting condition, so can be used interchangeably) is derived from the Greek and literally means 'below the cartilage' and originally referred to an area of the body encased by the lower ribs. This area, below the diaphragm, houses the liver and spleen.

We need not trace its history in any detail, but suffice to say that as late as the seventeenth century university educated physicians were still being trained in the old principles of humoural pathology. In this system there were four 'humours' which were intimately associated with the organs (liver and spleen) in the hypochondrium. It was an imbalance between these humours that led to illness, so the theory went.

These humours were called phlegm, blood, choler and black bile and from the beginning were not only associated with physical happenings in the body but also with temperamental characteristics as well. So to this day we speak of phlegmatic, sanguine, choleric and melancholic characters. Indeed another not so well known alternative name for hypochondriasis is atrabilious, which literally means 'black bile'.

However if this old theory is taken absolutely literally, one of the humours was bound to predominate so that perfect health was almost, by definition, unattainable. This derivation also accounts for the wider meaning of ill-humoured, not just lacking in a sense of humour but tetchy and difficult.

In medieval theory the balance of humours in the body was believed to fluctuate with the phases of the moon. The moon was thought to control the amount of moisture in the body, and as the brain was considered to be the moistest part of the body it was the most susceptible. This led to the notion of insanity as lunacy or being moonstruck.

Even though we no longer accept these theories, in many cases we still use the ancient terms. Looked at through modern eyes it all seems pretty silly, although we are not really as sophisticated as we like to think. For instance the continued popularity of horoscopes and the wearing of copper bracelets as protection against rheumatism.

Popular phrases, too, often help to perpetuate older ideas without our realizing it. For example we still talk about being 'liverish' meaning not only generally out of sorts, with biliousness and other unpleasant feelings, but also rather irritable as well. We also talk about being 'under the weather' and many a hypochondriac very much blames the climate, at least for some of his afflictions.

These ideas illustrate a very important theme which is still very relevant today in understanding illness. That is to see possible connections and interplay between bodily events, mental ones and environmental happenings.

It was not until the nineteenth century that hypochondria began to be used in a much more restricted sense, now beginning to mean a type of over-concern with health.

Unfortunately along with its more narrow medical usage there has also grown up a popular stereotype of what constitutes a hypochondriac. This really boils down to no more than calling someone you dislike by various unflattering names. In other words 'hypochondriac' can be a term of abuse.

In this popular misuse it is implied that the hypochondriac is an old fuss-pot, with nothing really wrong with him. He either imagines it all or grossly exaggerates minor aches and pains which everybody else ignores. He is seen as a nuisance, a time waster, attention seeking and always on about his health. A 'creaking gate' who nonetheless seems to keep remarkably well and will probably outlive us all. So the popular view runs, with the further implication that what he really needs is either ignoring, a kick up the backside or simply to pull himself together.

This is not, of course, what is implied when used medically. For those who read their doctors' letters this might come as a great shock (similar misunderstandings can result from other diagnostic terms like hysterical) when nothing of the sort is intended; it is the same word but here having a different, technical meaning. It, like all medical diagnoses, is a sort of technical short-hand enabling doctors to communicate with each other without having to go into lengthy explanations all the time. Having had a similar medical training they know what is meant. It is a convenient descriptive label but devoid of any personal criticism or notions of good or bad.

To get all this into proper perspective we need to know a little bit more about what constitutes health and ill-health and to realize that there is a vast range of what is considered to be normal. In practically everything that can be measured, from such things as height and weight to level of intelligence, there is no absolute normal but a considerable range.

Before doing that I would like you to know something more about various background factors which can influence people in seeing others as hypochondriacs.

## 2

## Complaining Types

Here I am concerned with some of the general characteristics of hypochondriacs and whether or not certain people
are more prone than others to suffer in this way. Clearly
the sort of person you are influences the way in which you
will react to different situations including being ill.

You may be the sort of person who thinks a lot, worries
a good deal but likes to keep things to yourself and not
get involved with others or want to bother them. If something is wrong with you, even though you may suffer as
much as the next man, you would rather 'grin and bear it'
and not make a fuss. In this case you will, less often than
some other types, become a complainer or get labelled a
hypochondriac.

On the other hand if you are a more outgoing type,
like meeting people and confiding in them, like a 'no
nonsense' approach and to call a spade a spade, you are
much more likely to tell others about your worries and
how you are feeling. This was certainly the case in one
investigation of women with a painful disease. Those who
were rated as being particularly outgoing but also highly
neurotic, complained much more and were given more
pain-killing drugs than the other women.

It is alleged that men are much more likely than women
to turn into hypochondriacs. Men may well react in a
more physical way and so come up more easily with bodily
symptoms. Women are more emotional creatures and may
well express themselves more in this way.

A picture is sometimes painted of different sorts of 'flu.
If dad gets it, he immediately takes to his bed, complains

loudly of a dreadful headache and how ill and sick he feels. He is quite unable to get about because of dizziness and weakness of his legs. He must have total peace and quiet, time off work and plenty of attention from a loving wife. When mum gets 'flu things are quite different. Then 'it's only 'flu'; a few aspirins are all that is needed to keep her going; she can still cope with the kids and get the meals ready and there is no great fuss and bother.

This may be a little unfair and partly the result of one of the many fixed ideas we have about how men and women behave. This is further illustrated by the sex incidence of hysteria when the boot is on the other foot. In other words just because you are a woman you stand a far higher chance of being called hysterical and just because you are a man, a hypochondriac. In reality the two conditions have much in common but it has become traditional to think about them in different ways, depending on the sex of the sufferer. (For more details of this see Chapter 6.)

In some respects women do seem to be tougher than men; the most obvious way is that, on average, women live longer, so that the 'geriatric problem' is largely a female one. Also women's toleration of discomfort and pain may well be different. They have their monthly periods and childbirth to put up with, so perhaps they soon learn to tolerate more pain before complaining about it. This is discussed in more detail in Chapter 4.

Another important factor is age, the very young and the old tending to be more hypochondriacal. This is understandable as the young are undergoing rapid changes in the process of growing up, which directs their attention to their appearance and bodily health. The young are still feeling their way in life, are dependent and unsure of themselves, and tend to get moody, self-centred and difficult. In a way this can all happen again in your 'second childhood', when increasing age may bring back similar problems of adjustment.

Naturally enough people in certain occupations tend to get more hypochondriacal than others. You can, for instance, imagine that medical students could get like this at times. Having to learn about all the different diseases for the first time and then coming into contact with patients actually suffering from them. The students themselves are still young, relatively inexperienced, often working under great stress, with important examinations and other worries to cope with as well. Others particularly prone are athletes, actors, opera singers and ballet dancers.

Certain races and nationalities seem to get a reputation for being hypochondriacs. This is nearly always the opinion of others, as we tend to make fun of or denigrate strangers and foreigners, in order to hide our inherent fear of them. At one time we ourselves had this reputation when in the seventeenth century and later it was referred to as 'The English Malady'. Hypochondria has taken different forms at different times in our history and certainly can attain peculiar forms in other cultures.

Of our European colleagues, the Italians, Germans and the French are currently popular contenders in the hypochondria stakes. The Germans worry a lot over their bowels and have an odd complaint of excessive tiredness in the Spring. The French are concerned about their livers and biliousness, this in many cases being realistic, as they have a high incidence of liver disease associated with alcoholism.

Some hypochondriacal complaints are entirely 'culture bound', that is, they only occur in a certain group of people. An interesting example of this is the case of the disappearing penis! This condition, called Koro, is found almost exclusively amongst certain groups of Chinese and fits in with their folk beliefs. The sufferer firmly believes his penis is shrinking and will eventually disappear inside his body. He may try and prevent this by putting a peg on it or getting his womenfolk to hang on to it!

Indians, too, seem to be particularly prone to hypochondriacal worries, especially over their virility and potency. Finally Jews also have a reputation for being hypochondriacal; perhaps it is in their nature to be rather excitable and body conscious.

Generally speaking both relatively unsophisticated societies and individuals seem more prone to produce physical symptoms than psychological ones like anxiety or depression. Their fears and worries are given a more concrete physical form such as complaints of sweating and trembling rather than feeling anxious or insecure. But we must bear in mind that many deprived and underprivileged societies do in fact suffer from more physical illness anyway, such as infections, as a result of malnutrition and poor living conditions.

In our own society we can see a similar tendency, when hypochondriacal complaints seem to be more frequent in those from the larger and poorer families, who perhaps, also lack the necessary education to understand themselves better or express themselves in any other way.

It follows, too, that if you have mistaken or odd ideas about your body, based on old wives' tales and family traditions, this will make you more vulnerable to hypochondriacal worries. If you believe that you must have your bowels opened at least once every day ('an apple a day keeps the doctor away') or else poisons will build up in your system and you'll become ill with bad breath and a blotchy skin, then if you do miss a day you'll start getting upset.

Your beliefs about and your attitudes towards your body and health in general, are important influences. We are, of course, all products of our own society and tend to reflect the wider ideas and beliefs of that particular section of society from which we come. This is partly passed on to us by our upbringing and by other educational influences in childhood and later life.

A big influence nowadays is advertising, especially on television. The young are vulnerable to this and so are very open to commercial exploitation. In turn they are very much influenced by each other, in respect of how they look, their make-up and clothes. So many advertisements are designed to start you thinking about germs, hygiene, drains, lavatories, bad breath, body odour, and such like. When these are coupled with pictures of romantic rewards if you do the right thing (i.e. buy the product advertised), with social embarrassment and rejection if you don't, it can all be very persuasive. Fortunately some people are more resistant than others.

What is considered to be 'illness' or something else like wickedness, delinquency or divine judgement, is largely determined by current fashion, which is subject to change. This also applies to what should be done about it; whether treatment, punishment, nature cure, spiritual guidance or whatever, is most appropriate.

In our own society today there seem to be two general trends. The first is fostered by the idea of the Welfare State and a comprehensive free National Health Service. In this sort of outlook the idea is there should be no suffering or unhappiness, there is a pill for every pain, with stoicism and the stiff upper lip seen as old-fashioned. The other general trend is for soldiering on, taking pride in your own self-sufficiency and not bothering others, including doctors, unless absolutely necessary.

In some ways you can't win. If you keep going to your doctor at the drop of a hat, you're a hypochondriac. If you don't, yet keep on complaining about various symptoms, others will think you can't be that bad otherwise you wouldn't be working or going out. So again you could be said to be making a lot of fuss about nothing, and therefore a hypochondriac!

One fashionable trend at the moment is to get right away from conventional medical ideas and ask not what is wrong with you, how are you feeling or what's the matter but why do you behave in this way? Terms like the 'sick role' or 'illness behaviour' are bandied about. This sort of approach implies that such behaviour has been learnt and is to be seen more like a bad habit or way of life rather than in the usual medical way of looking at an illness. The 'medical model' is of an illness with a well defined cause, such as a bug, certain pathological changes in the body, and a predictable course and outcome.

A further implication of the 'behavioural' approach is that the reason you behave in this way now, and how you behave in other situations, is very much bound up with the sort of person you are.

Another important factor highlighted by this way of looking at hypochondriacal behaviour is to remind us that there are certain advantages to be had from being sick. In some ways it's like going back to being a child again. You are no longer expected to cope with your normal responsibilities and others take over your care and management. This obviously has certain attractions, especially if your life is going through a bad patch at the time.

But again different people react differently to the same situation; some will welcome it and find it very difficult to get going again. Others, who are fiercely independent types will often regard it as 'giving in', a sign of weakness or incompetence. With this may go a lot of resentment, if you finally have to 'give in', at being less efficient than usual and losing your independence and control over things. This may make you a 'difficult' patient, but only too happy to be standing on your own two feet again as soon as possible.

Society by and large likes people to fall into well defined categories, with definite rules and expectations of how you should behave in various situations. You are either ill or well. Unfortunately there are many 'grey' areas in between, and many people don't fit into some neat, black or white, official classification. Being a hypochondriac is a case in point. So much easier if you are covered in bandages or have your arm in a sling, everyone then understands the situation and behaves accordingly.

How you actually make your complaints is also influenced by your background. At the best of times it's difficult to put rather vague feelings into words. It seems so much easier and apparently more easily understood by others, to say you feel ill in a more precise physical way.

Also to whom you make your complaints is similarly influenced. After all you yourself have to make the initial decision as to how you feel, what you think might be the matter and to whom, if anybody, you should go to about it.

To sum up so far. You are not alone, we all have the capacity to become hypochondriacs and many of us do, at least for short periods of time, suffer in this way. But the sort of person you are and your background are important influences in determining what form your illness takes, how you react to it and what you do about it.

# 3

# Good Health

In this chapter I want to discuss what we mean by both good and bad health. More detailed accounts of some of the points raised will be taken up again in later chapters.

First, good health. You may say why waste time on this, isn't it obvious when I'm healthy, I feel fine and have no complaints about my health. This is true, up to a point, even though it is surprisingly difficult to give a definition of good health. It is not entirely negative, simply the absence of disease but should include a positive sense of well-being too.

Obviously in planning health services it would be nice to know just how many sick people there are in the community, what they are suffering from and following from this, what sort of treatment facilities are needed. This is much harder to do than you might suppose. You need some sort of agreement in advance as to what constitutes a 'case' of illness and how to measure this. This is difficult enough to do even for common everyday illnesses but even more so, for instance, in trying to give an estimate as to the number of hypochondriacs there are in the community. Also to answer the seemingly reasonable question, are they on the increase or not?

The following statement appeared in a medical journal:

Conservatively speaking, patients with primary hypochondriacal symptoms or hypochondriacal overlay superimposed upon minor somatic disorders represent more than 50 per cent of all patients seen by physicians, general practitioners and specialists alike.

But how can they be so sure and how was this measured?

Apart from trying to see how many people seem to fit the general definition of a hypochondriac I have already given you at the beginning of this book, how else could it be done?

Various attempts have been made, both here and in America to draw up questionnaires and lists requiring the answers (sometimes a simple yes or no) to various questions about how you are feeling and whether you have certain specified complaints about your mental and physical health. The answers are then put into the form of a score or sometimes put through very elaborate mathematical processes, with some cut-off point, above which you are a hypochondriac but below which you are not.

These attempts at measurement have not been very successful (although they can provide useful pointers for further research) for reasons already mentioned as well as the fact that there are several different types of hypochondriac anyway. The wider issue of what is meant by being mentally healthy or not, is also raised by this sort of approach.

Before giving you some idea of the different sorts of mental disorders that are usually recognized, and where hypochondriacs can be fitted into such a scheme, I would first like to mention current ideas about mental health. You often meet terms like 'mature', 'well-adjusted' and 'psychologically healthy', but what do these really mean?

As regards maturity it is easier to understand what is meant by immaturity. You are immature when you think, feel or behave in a way which is more appropriate to an earlier stage of development. Actually the person who was one hundred per cent mature the whole time would be quite insufferable. We all behave immaturely on occasions; it is when you are like this for most of the time that we are concerned with, that is, having an immature personality.

Looking at it from the other end, there are certain general qualities which you, as a mature person, should have, such as a sense of personal identity with a reasonable estimate of your abilities, limitations and faults. Secondly a sympathetic appreciation of the claims and rights of others. Thirdly an ability to balance these interests when they come into conflict so that you can make effective decisions taking into account both immediate consequences as well as long-term effects.

In general terms if you are a well-adjusted person it means being able to provide for such fundamental needs as adequate food, warmth and shelter. To respond to the moral and legal codes of your society allowing for the fact that ours is a very complicated one so it will contain some inconsistencies. That means that even a well-adjusted person may be in conflict with some sets of principles.

Once these adjustments have been coped with there still remain a number of needs which each of us experiences and must do something about, such as the need for self-esteem, independence from others, the need for personal security in the form of the esteem of others and recognition of our achievements. Satisfaction of these different kinds of need involves compromises and conflicts which we all try to solve in our own individual ways. The different ways of solving such conflicts will express our different types of personality.

Another way of looking at all this is to ask, am I normal? There are unfortunately, several different meanings of this word. One is the same as average, with a normal range of distribution. When tested on intelligence tests the majority of the general population get an I.Q. score between 75–125, the normal distribution of intelligence. In this instance it would be abnormal to be either a genius or mentally defective.

Normal does not necessarily mean healthy, as it is normal in this (average) sense to suffer from tooth decay, but hardly healthy. We have already noted the difficulties in measuring hypochondria and counting how many hypochondriacs there are. These things do not lend themselves very well to being counted. Indeed some attempts to measure how much mental ill-health there is in the population have come up with some surprising results. One American survey found up to 70 per cent of the population surveyed had psychiatric symptoms, so that here 'normal' would in fact be unhealthy. But abnormal can be used in another way, simply to equate it with unhealthy, morbid or disease ridden.

A final way of looking at mental health is once again to bring the environment into it, both the internal one of your mind and body as well as the outside world around you. Mental health could then be defined as a harmonious relationship between self and environment.

Having said all this, there are two general characteristics of any illness. These are pain or suffering and loss of efficiency. These can certainly occur as part of a hypochondriacal illness. But we need to get away from a too narrow medical view of illness to understand more fully just why you suffer in this particular way. Disease written dis-ease suggests a much more general upset of the whole person, which is frequently the case.

You will probably have heard of some conditions being referred to as 'psychosomatic'. This means a physical disorder, such as asthma, whose nature can only be fully understood by taking into account emotional factors as well as physical ones. Sometimes these illnesses are called 'stress disorders' and we certainly hear a lot about the stresses of modern life.

Used medically 'stress' is really derived from 'distress' and refers not to obvious major calamities like an earthquake but to much more personal and subtle ones, usually involving relationships with other people, like loss of an important relationship in bereavement, separation or divorce or loss of face or self-esteem. After all we often say so-and-so gives me a pain in the neck or makes me sick, and this can happen quite literally. So that 'stress' is a very individual matter and what may be stressful for you could act as a challenge and a spur to try harder in somebody else. But such stresses can play a big part in either turning you into a hypochondriac in the first place or in keeping you that way.

Mental stress can even make you more liable to catch infectious conditions (probably by altering the hormones and various bodily defences) such as the common cold. Indeed it often seems that when you hit a bad patch in your life and have a lot of worries, you become more prone to all sorts of illnesses, psychological, physical and psychosomatic, which seem to come in clusters. Everything happens at once.

How well integrated you are in the society in which you live is also important for your health. It's not so much the physical conditions under which you work and live, important though they are, but how well you get on with your family, neighbours, workmates, and other groups. Do you feel you belong, have a place in the scheme of things and feel part of a much larger group? Frequent moves, coming from a very different culture, never growing any roots or always being at odds with everyone around you, all these can produce a state of stressful conflict.

Many of the resulting illnesses are fluctuating ones, and if you, and indeed, your doctor, can find the answers to four rather simple questions, you have gone a very long way in understanding your condition. The first question is, why did you start to get ill when you did? In other words look for stressful factors that may have occurred during the preceding weeks and months. These are often cumulative, in that individually they didn't seem very serious, but coming fairly rapidly one on top of another they can be very stressful indeed.

The second question is a bit more difficult. Why are you hypochondriacal in this particular way and not in another? Why, for example, are you always worried by headaches and the possibility of a brain tumour and not indigestion and your bowels? It could be because headaches run in your family, or you've had a previous injury or illness involving your head, perhaps in childhood, or this part of your body had special significance for you.

The third question involves finding out just what sort of a person you really are, your personality and temperament, and what kind of a life you have had. There will be more about this aspect in a later chapter. The fourth and last question is rather like the first one, only in reverse. Why did you get better when you did?

Let us now consider what other types of mental disorder there are, particularly ones with hypochondriacal symptoms. There are a group of disorders, extremely common, called neurotic, but watch out again for this name being misused. Used technically and not popularly a neurotic is a person who shows persistently inadequate reactions to circumstances so that in one way or another he just cannot cope with life. In this sense we are all potential neurotics and can all be 'inadequate' at times.

Some general characteristics of a neurosis are that it is firmly rooted in normality and bears a close relationship to the sort of person you are (personality) but still leaves you with both feet on the ground. You usually realize something is wrong with you and it is relatively easy for others to put themselves in your shoes, as we have all felt something like this on occasions.

Common forms of neurotic illness are anxiety states which are sometimes accompanied by phobias (Chapter 5), depression (Chapter 7), hysteria (Chapter 6) and obsessional neurosis (Chapter 9).

In the rather more serious 'nervous breakdown' or psychotic illness (Chapter 8) contact with the real world may well be lost. You may no longer care about the world anyway, or even become so worried and withdrawn that you live in an entirely different world of your own. You imagine that people are talking about you behind your back, or you see 'pictures on the wall' or hear things that no one else can hear. Fears may now turn into firm convictions, in spite of all evidence to the contrary.

Even though it is said that when you reach this stage you don't even realize you're ill and others find it difficult to understand you as the feelings and experiences you have are so extraordinary, this is not always so by any means. Nor is it strictly true to say no ordinary person has ever felt like this. In one sense we all go 'mad' every night, in our dreams and nightmares, and indeed this sort of illness can be very like having a nightmare only when you are fully awake during the daytime.

There is finally a group of people who in many respects are not strictly speaking ill but have underdeveloped or immature personalities, lopsided ones (e.g. born worriers or highly strung) or who show other exaggerated features like violent mood swings or very aggressive or suspicious tendencies. There are those, too, who by nature are both body and health conscious and so prone to behave in a hypochondriacal way. People with these disorders of their personality (further details in Chapter 9) are very vulnerable, when under stress, to develop into caricatures of what they are usually like. The 'born worrier', for instance, will very easily develop an anxiety neurosis. So you can see that the more abnormal or unusual your personality the less stress it takes to throw you off balance and make you ill.

When we come to take an overall view of how these various illnesses and reactions are caused you will appreciate it is often a complicated matter, with not one simple clear-cut cause, but a lot of them, very often ending up over a period of time in some sort of vicious circle.

As we've already seen, much depends on your constitution, the sort of person you are both physically and emotionally, which in turn depends to a certain extent on characteristics inherited from your parents, as well as how you were brought up. Not only this but you should also consider what other experiences in your life could have contributed to your present troubles. These may be either physical, social or emotional. Finally more recent stresses may put the cap on it, so that some form of neurotic illness is the end result.

I hope enough has been said to show you that, although often complicated, and of course people are, the position is rarely so complicated that the various details cannot be worked out and understood. This also points to possible remedies. Even if you can't alter past events, you at least may be able to take a fresh look at them. You can certainly alter your present feelings and attitudes and try to do something about the present and immediate future.

# 4

## Types of Complaint

There are obviously many different types of complaint which you could have, either singly or in combination. So many that I can't possibly cover them all. Instead I would like to make some general observations with particular emphasis on painful symptoms. Doctors themselves do talk about 'complaints' but more often call them symptoms, so that we can use the names interchangeably.

From my own examination of the records of several hundred hypochondriacs, it was possible to see several patterns which kept on recurring. One of these was the part of the body that was most commonly affected. Most complaints centred on the region of the head and neck followed by the abdomen and then the chest. Looking at these symptoms from the point of view of which tissues were most often affected, the muscles, joints and bones headed the list. The digestive tract (stomach, gut and bowels) came second and the nervous system third.

A smaller group of patients was carefully investigated in hospital when under half were found to have a significant physical disease that could account for some of the symptoms. Other very common general symptoms were depression, tiredness, weakness and anxiety.

In a few hypochondriacs there is one major outstanding symptom which overshadows all others, often a painful one, like backache. This may take you to all sorts of different doctors in the hope of finding a cure. More common are those who have a number of different complaints. Sometimes these are very diffuse and vague, which makes it difficult for you to point to which part of your body seems to be affected, as well as making it hard to put into words and describe for somebody else to understand. This can make you feel quite desperate at times.

In all the cases which have been studied, both by general practitioners and specialists, there is one very important symptom which constantly appears and that is discomfort or pain.

Now pain is Nature's warning sign that something is wrong but there are different sorts of pain pointing to different causes. How pain is felt is surprisingly complicated and in one sense it is 'all in the mind' or at least the brain, as it is here that we actually appreciate that a sensation is painful.

If you have a painful knee the sensation is carried up to the brain by special nerve fibres, where they are then sorted out and recognized as painful by the conscious mind. If the pain is very severe other symptoms like faintness, sweating and a feeling of sickness often accompany it. Even though pain is a warning sign, not all illnesses are painful, at least to begin with. A routine chest X-ray may pick out the very early stages of a disease, which has not yet produced any symptoms, a so-called silent focus.

One thing is certain, you can't imagine a pain; you've either got one or you haven't. However the feeling of pain can be 'postponed' if you are under a great strain or other powerful emotion at the time. Examples would be in the middle of an exciting game, during a battle or during very pleasant experiences which may 'compete' for attention. You may have a bad pain in the chest which gets worse when you exert yourself but which you may hardly notice during sexual intercourse.

Pain can, of course, be exaggerated or described in a way that makes other people think you're putting it on a bit. A person who is naturally rather histrionic may

21

describe a pain in a rather theatrical way, but nonetheless suffers just the same. One of the ways in which emotion can actually induce pain is by rapid overbreathing, panting very rapidly and violently through your mouth, rather like a dog does in hot weather. This alters the composition of the blood and can cause pins and needles as well as painful muscle cramps in the limbs. Some very excitable or nervous people indulge in this overbreathing without being fully aware of what they are doing.

Pain is not always felt in the place from which it originates; this is called 'referred pain'. For instance stomach pain may be felt in the chest or pain from the heart in the left shoulder. This is because many internal organs cannot themselves react to pain, so nerve messages are passed back to those bodily areas from which they developed before birth.

It is not always easy to say exactly what we mean by mental pain. Even if we can't define it we know what we mean when we say to somebody who's been nasty to us 'you've hurt my feelings'. Think, too, of the occasion when you don't want to tell someone you no longer love them, in case you hurt them. No physical pain or injury is intended. What we are really talking about is grief, suffering, feelings of rejection, humiliation and depression. All very real and 'painful'.

After a time it's sometimes difficult to tell the cart from the horse, as after all what can be more demoralizing and depressing than to be in constant pain. So you will see that pain is always both mental and physical.

The trouble is that pain is difficult to measure, being such a subjective experience. Your reactions to a pain may be very different from somebody else's. Indeed you may have a different pain threshold, a certain level above which sensations are definitely interpreted as being painful. Also how well or badly you actually tolerate pain and how you complain about it, are again very individual matters.

We have already noted that more introverted people tend to complain less readily than more outgoing types and hinted at some sex differences. But social pressures, attitudes and expectations also have a bearing on this. You may behave quite differently, when in pain, when on your own in the privacy of your own home than you would in a busy, public hospital ward.

We still tend to treat boys and girls rather differently; girls are allowed to cry and express their feelings more openly than boys, who are made to feel cissy or bad if they do so. This stiff upper lip approach, if carried to extremes, can result in the sort of person who becomes scared of his emotions and learns to keep the 'lid on' and bottle everything up. But all this churned-up emotion must escape somehow and one way it does so is to come out in the form of symptoms, especially painful ones.

In one study it was found that male patients reckoned they had experienced more severe pain more often than female patients and they complained about it and asked for pain-killing drugs more often. However the all female nursing staff actually gave the men less painkilling medication than they gave the women and often gave it to the women without being asked. So you will see that because the staff expected the men to complain more often, they did. The men also felt the staff were not free enough about giving them the drugs, so they asked for them sooner and more often. On the other hand the women showed more trust and felt the staff would be aware of their needs, so did not need to complain as much as the men did.

Age is another factor; it often seems that very young children are able to bounce back from all sorts of falls and injuries without apparently suffering much pain. However certain pains in children, such as recurrent abdominal ones, may well be partly caused or prolonged by emotional upsets. A lot depends on how you are brought up. Certain 'traditions' seem to run in families, like headaches or period pains. Too much may have been made of them and you subsequently learn, often without realizing it, that this is one way of gaining attention and love, and a way of communicating with others. This may be especially so in very large families.

If you are a very uptight, tense sort of person, a worrier who takes life very seriously, then you can be prone to not only getting your whole body tensed up but individual groups of muscles as well. So that this, perhaps in some cases combined with bad posture, can result in pain. Feelings of guilt, unexpressed anger and sexual conflicts can all be important background factors as well.

A pain may be prolonged because it has almost become a habit or way of life which carries its own rewards, as in the idea of the 'sick role' already mentioned. You may find it easier, yes less painful, to blame all your failures and personal inadequacies not on yourself but on your painful condition. If only I didn't have this pain I would be able to go out, meet people, find a girlfriend, leave home and get a good job. It is understandably easier to say this rather than, I'm shy, unsure of myself, I can't really stand on my own two feet yet and I need further support and protection, someone to lean on. This is not to be confused with frank malingering, which is extremely rare.

Diffuse aches and pains are common and are often put down to 'rheumatism', 'fibrositis', 'growing pains' or living in a damp house, when they could well be more an expression of how frustrating and difficult you find life and how unhappy you are. That these sometimes get better simply by wearing a copper bracelet or some other charm with no proven scientific value, shows that emotional factors can have some influence.

You may be a sufferer from rheumatoid arthritis, which can cause painful swellings of the joints, especially the smaller ones, or arthritis of one of your larger joints. Much depends on your personality and your life circumstances how you take such an illness and whether or not you sink into a state of hypochondriacal depression.

Common 'localized' pains, which can cause a great deal of hypochondriacal concern, are headaches and pains in the face, neck, chest, back, abdomen and pelvis.

The typical tension headache, as the name suggests, is caused by anxiety and tension, and is quite different from migraine although both may occur in similar people. Nonetheless if your headaches persist or constantly recur you may start to worry in case you've got something nasty like a brain tumour. In which case the further worry will only make the headaches worse. 'Eyestrain' very rarely causes headaches nor does high blood pressure.

Facial pain may be attributed to sinusitis, dental troubles or to disease of one of the nerves to the area. Occasionally the whole thing occurs in a setting of mental depression and responds to anti-depressant treatment.

Wax in the ear rarely causes any problems but you may find that you get into the habit of picking at your ears with your finger nails, which can cause soreness. The frequent use of ear drops should be avoided. Worries over increasing deafness and failing eyesight may or may not be justified. Postponement of wearing glasses or a hearing aid may be due not so much to vanity but to a denial of increasing age.

'Floaters' or little specks in front of the eyes, seen more clearly on looking at a plain white surface or a clear blue sky, are normal, we all have them. Only sometimes when you get worried and turn in on yourself you notice them for the first time. In fact if you start paying attention to any part of your body or any function that usually goes on automatically, like blinking or breathing, it immediately starts to go haywire. Constantly rubbing your eyes when you feel there is something in them only makes them red and even sorer.

A lump in the throat can also be a sign of emotional disturbance, but if food seems to stick or there is real difficulty in swallowing, a doctor should be consulted. Recurrent 'catarrh', sore throats and sinusitis may get blamed on the weather, allergies, a bug or any combination of these. If you are inclined to be hypochondriacal anyway, any of these complaints can become the focus of endless worries. Sometimes the condition is perpetuated by bad habits, like wrongly blowing your nose. Do not block up one nostril and blow as hard as you can down the other one to try and unblock it; gently blow through both nostrils at the same time.

We have already mentioned somebody being 'a pain in the neck' and you can think of other expressions which make the neck important emotionally. For instance 'necking' and 'sticking your neck out'. There are a number of prominent muscles here, going to the back of the head and shoulders, so that stiffness and various pains in the region are quite frequent and such conditions as 'wry neck' can result. Occasionally pain and limited movement is due to changes in the bones of the neck rather than the muscles.

The chest is also of great emotional significance because of associations with the heart, breath and breasts. Chest pains are a constant source of worry, particularly in men, as so much publicity has been given in recent years to coronary heart disease. Is it only indigestion, something I've eaten, too much gardening, an impending stroke or heart attack? Such frightening thoughts may well occur to you when you experience chest pain in the middle of the night. Should you call a doctor, take an aspirin or what? There are many possible causes of chest pain from cramp and a cracked rib to chronic bronchitis.

Before we go on to consider other possible causes of chest pain, let us look at some recent research findings about coronary heart disease in order to help you understand both the underlying causes and the modern approach to treatment.

First of all, the name itself, what is actually meant by 'a coronary'? The heart is basically a pump, the walls of which are made of muscle. Like any other sort of muscle, particularly such an active one, it needs a good blood supply to keep working properly. The small arteries which supply the heart muscle itself are called the coronary vessels and it's when these get blocked that the trouble starts and the heart is no longer able to function as an efficient pump.

It is now realized that it is not just a simple matter of leading a very stressful life that will do this. There are a whole range of other factors which can also be relevant—called risk factors. These include a family history of similar heart trouble, being overweight, having a high blood pressure, not taking enough exercise, smoking cigarettes, eating the wrong food and having a certain type of personality.

The type of person most vulnerable is the 'work addict' or 'tycoon type'. That is someone who is highly competitive, aggressive, restless, impatient, always feeling under pressure, with a ceaseless striving for achievement and an overdedication to the job. It's as if you were always seeking power, perhaps as a substitute for some other emotional satisfaction such as love.

Stress, anxiety and sometimes even prolonged grief can actually cause a coronary by raising the level of certain fatty substances such as cholesterol, in the blood, which then accumulate in and clog up the small coronary arteries. Other factors are constant high blood pressure stretching and damaging the walls of the arteries and the release of other chemical substances which cause the heart to beat too vigorously. When a coronary artery gets completely clogged up, the piece of muscle which it supplies stops working. It is possible to die literally from a broken heart, as sometimes happens during the first year after being widowed.

You may have heard of people dying from a heart attack during their sleep (surely a nice way to go and not to be feared) but yet this is just the time when you are supposed to be completely at rest. As you will see later on, there are different sorts of sleep, one sort being associated with increased blood pressure, heart rate and even the release of more fatty substances into the blood stream.

When you think, though, of all the possible risk factors that can lead to a coronary, you will realize that a number of them can be modified, so that you can help yourself in either preventing it happening in the first place, or coming on again. Obvious ways are to give up smoking cigarettes, get your weight down and eat a sensible diet. But what sort of a diet? For this you need to cut down on fat, which you get mainly from meat, dairy products, margarine, cooking fats, cakes and pastries. A small reduction in all these could lead to a considerable reduction in total fat intake.

More specifically, you should avoid saturated fats by eating fewer egg yokes and less meat; grill rather than fry, and eat more poultry and fish. Avoid cream and the top of the milk. Use a soft margarine and oils rich in polyunsaturated fats for cooking, e.g. corn oil. Oils labelled merely 'vegetable oil' may contain a good deal of saturated fat and very little polyunsaturated, and should be avoided. Eat more vegetables, and fruit of all kinds. Although the exact mode of action is unknown, there is a strong association with soft drinking water, which should be avoided as far as possible.

Some modification of your whole way of life can also be attempted, especially if you are chronically anxious and the striving sort already mentioned. On the other hand, just because you are a worrying type or hypochondriacal about your heart, does not necessarily mean you are bound to develop a coronary.

Another clue to prevention is the fact that women, at least young women, seem to be relatively free from this type of heart attack. This is shown most readily by the protective influence of pregnancy and by the fact that women who do get a coronary are mostly past the change of life.

Various reasons have been suggested for this (and indeed for the different incidence of other psychosomatic conditions like duodenal ulcer). Perhaps it has something to do with the protective influence of the female sex hormones (oestrogens) or the fact that women have different sex chromosomes. Also, at least up to quite recently, women smoked fewer cigarettes, generally led a different sort of life and perhaps too, had a rather different diet. For whatever reasons women seem to have much lower levels of fatty substances in their blood than men.

It could be that the crucial differences really lie in up-bringing and cultural factors. Men have traditionally been the hunters, the competitive, aggressive go-getters and bread winners. They have consequently been subjected to the full blast of all the stresses and strains of a modern industrialized society (coronary disease is anyway relatively rare in non-industrialized societies). Rapid changes in male and female roles, particularly in women becoming more independent, have also brought undesirable effects, for example men have the further upset of having to cope with different attitudes and behaviour of their wives and children. Also for women, there is an increasing incidence of what have traditionally been male type stress disorders, such as heart disease and ulcers.

But left-sided chest pain can occur which has nothing to do with angina or any serious physical condition, as part of what has been called the 'effort syndrome'. This is a neurotic disorder, commoner in women, and with a characteristic sort of pain. The pain can occur anytime, especially when you are tired but effort is limited by exhaustion rather than by pain itself. The pain is generally continuous and can last weeks or months, with a gradual onset. It can spread and there may be a tender area round the original site of the pain. Other symptoms are usually present as well, such as palpitations and a feeling of not ever being able to really fill the lungs with a satisfying deep breath of air.

In the vertical scheme of the body there are three focal points, brain, heart and sexual organs, with the central point being the heart. Its obvious emotional significance is highlighted by the tremendous interest shown in heart transplant operations, with no public interest in the equally revolutionary liver transplants. The heart symbolizes life itself, as well as love and the emotions generally.

It is only too easy to develop a neurosis about your heart. You may have had rheumatic fever as a child and a lot of fuss made of you at the time in case it affected your heart. You may have been coddled at school and restricted in playing games and taking exercise. You may have been told you have a 'tired heart' or to be 'careful' after a routine medical examination when the doctor heard an unusual heart sound (murmur). Even if you have angina or have had a minor heart attack, your life can be made a misery by too many restrictions, leaving you in constant dread of another attack.

Other heart symptoms, such as palpitations—your heart seeming to miss a beat or 'turn over', start racing or thumping—are nearly always entirely due to emotional causes like anxiety and not serious heart disease. You should not always be feeling your pulse or heart beat or worrying over your blood pressure; anxious hypochondriacal concern will only make things worse.

Low back pain is another common complaint. It may have started as a strain or you may have been told you've injured a disc or bruised your spine. There are so many muscles in your back that they are practically uncountable and they, too, can be subject to tension and the backache seeming very much worse when you are depressed or anxious.

As with all these pains they can be used as excuses to avoid other activities, such as sexual intercourse, perhaps without your fully realizing what you are doing. If compensation is involved, say following an industrial accident and it's a long drawn out procedure, it's not surprising that emotional factors also get involved.

Abdominal pain may be associated with indigestion, biliousness, wind or occasionally an ulcer. Sometimes you feel very bloated and in need of bringing up some wind. In the process of trying to do this you may well swallow a lot of air, which only distends you further. A feeling of sinking or butterflies in the pit of the stomach is due to anxiety, which can also cause feelings of sickness.

Various surveys of people suffering from indigestion have shown that about 80 per cent have no serious physical illness. You may have heard of 'acid indigestion' or having too much acid in your stomach, as if there shouldn't be any there at all. You do, in fact, need acid in order to digest your food properly—this is quite normal—but it may get too concentrated, be produced in too large amounts or at inappropriate times when there is no food to digest. It may also get into other parts of the digestive system where it shouldn't be.

The gullet or oesophagus is joined onto the top of the stomach and sometimes there is a weakness at this junction, so that acid from the stomach comes up into the gullet and causes heartburn (nothing to do with the heart!). The stomach empties into the duodenum, and again acid seems to be one important factor in causing a duodenal ulcer.

Doctors talk about peptic ulcers, meaning either gastric (stomach) or duodenal ulcers, of which there are several different varieties, and possible complications. Most of these ulcers can be shown up on X-rays after you have swallowed a special drink containing barium, and it is this test which your doctor will recommend if he thinks you really have an ulcer.

A lot of recent research has shown us that previous, rather simple views both about how ulcers are caused and should be treated, need revising. As with other 'psychosomatic conditions' as we have already noted with coronary heart disease, there are interesting sex differences in their incidence. Peptic ulcers are still relatively common conditions although on the decline, and much more common in men; gastric ulcers are twice as common as in women, and duodenal ulcers, seven times more common.

As I am sure you will now realize there is no one simple cause, but a multitude of factors. In trying to understand these it may help to imagine the lining of the stomach and duodenum as a battlefield, with certain defences protecting it from attack and ulceration, with various substances and conditions trying to break it down. All sorts of things can upset this rather delicate balance and cause ulcers, such as aspirins, burns, injuries to the brain, some hormones and stressful experiences of all kinds. Ulcers can also be experimentally produced in animals, such as rats, dogs and monkeys.

One very famous experiment involved making monkeys into 'executives' which caused them to develop ulcers. Two lots of monkeys received electric shocks; one was tied up and was quite helpless; the other could, by learning to press a bar, avoid getting electric shocks both to itself and the one tied up in the same cage. It was the monkeys who had to make the decisions, whether or not to press the bar, (the 'executives') who developed the ulcers and not the ones who were completely passive and couldn't do anything about it.

There was, however, a fallacy in the way these 'executive' monkeys were chosen in the first place. It was done by simply taking the first four monkeys who were the quickest to learn the trick of pressing the bar. So they were a very select group and might well have been especially prone to develop ulcers in the first place; that is the quickest learners could be the most 'neurotic' and predisposed to get ulcers anyway.

In the comparable human situation, it may not be the executive's difficult job as such which produces his ulcers, it could be that the type of person who is prone to get ulcers for other reasons might also be the sort of person to land himself in a responsible executive type job. Nor is it, of course, only executives who get ulcers; for instance long distance lorry drivers may be equally likely.

It is not really possible to produce hypochondriacal animals, but clues can be got from animal experiments, about the possible roles of stress, fear and conflict, in producing ulcers. Another experiment showed rather different results from the monkey one, this time using rats. Rats were put into three different situations. In the first they were put into a restraining harness, given shocks, but with a warning they were coming and which they could avoid by making a certain response. In the second, the situation was the same except responses were ineffective in avoiding shocks. In the third they were similarly restrained but received no shocks.

It was the rats in the second situation who developed the most severe stomach ulcers. The general lesson from these experiments seems to be that fear aroused by physical pain depends on whether or not the pain is under the subject's control.

That emotions can affect the human stomach has been proved by direct observation. There have been one or two famous but unfortunate individuals who had developed holes in their stomach walls so that the lining of the stomach could be directly observed. They were then made angry or anxious, when the stomach lining would go red or white, and the stomach itself go into violent movements or pour out a lot of acid.

How this happens is another matter. There are, of course, nerves to the stomach, some of which do seem to be particularly concerned with acid secretion. These can be cut, in one sort of operation, to improve certain ulcers. It is also known that damage to particular areas of the brain, at least in animals, can lead to both gastric and duodenal ulcers. There are also some hormones, produced both locally in the stomach and more remotely in the brain, which can also affect both stomach movements and acid secretion.

Further animal experiments have also suggested that too early separation from the mother, living in very over-crowded conditions and other early environmental happenings can also predispose to the later development of ulcers. But we have to take all this animal work with a pinch of salt when we come to the vastly more complicated human situation.

It is unlikely that any one personality type is bound

to develop ulcers. We have already touched on this with the executive type. It could also of course, be his way of life, as well as his personality, that does the damage. For instance, hurried and irregular meals, smoking too much, drinking too much and so on. For reasons which are not fully understood, ulcers also seem to get worse in the Autumn and Spring.

One theory about personality type got round the difficulty of saying it was specific to a certain type of person by suggesting it was the inner (unconscious) conflicts that were specific. These could occur in outwardly very different sorts of people. This theory comes from psychoanalysts, and in their jargon hinges on 'oral dependency needs'. This means dealing with insecurity and inner conflicts by stuffing things into your mouth like food, cigarettes, drink, drugs or sweets. Like the baby who needs his comforter, either a dummy, his thumb or some other object he likes to suck—all ultimately substitutes for the breast and mother's milk.

It was suggested that men with duodenal ulcers had a persistent underlying conflict between infantile dependency needs— to be cared for, loved, nourished and protected—and the demands of adult life, when you can't be passive and dependent. This conflict was alleged to cause chronic oversecretion in the stomach. When, for some reason, this conflict became intensified (shall we say because of difficulties at work and home at the same time) it could then be either responsible for causing an ulcer or for a relapse in one already established. It was held that this actually came about via the nerves to the stomach that helped to control acid secretion.

The trouble with this theory, and many other similar ones derived from psychoanalysis, is that wide claims are made on the basis of the analysis of a very few, highly selected patients. The ideas got from those select few are then held to apply to everyone with an ulcer. Also inner (unconscious) conflicts are difficult to measure, prove or disprove, so that they cannot be put through rigorous scientific tests. It seems to me too, that most of us, at least at times, need to be dependent and babyish, and frequently are, yet we do not necessarily develop ulcers!

Undoubtedly though, anxiety can prolong or even cause a relapse in an ulcer and may even make complications more likely. It has been shown that the ulcers of patients who show persistent anxiety symptoms are much more likely to become chronic. And in a group of ulcer patients who were followed up over a number of years, it was noted that the presence of anxiety or depression at the outset, tended to go with a poor outlook for the ulcer healing.

But having said all that, it is still difficult to explain why the incidence of duodenal ulcer is declining; there is still plenty of stress about, and many neurotic people.

Nevertheless, an important part of the treatment of ulcers, apart from all the various medical and surgical measures which are currently available, is to avoid as far as possible, further hypochondriacal worries. You may worry in case it is cancer and not a simple ulcer, especially if you are in a lot of pain, can't eat or sleep properly, have lost weight or have either vomited blood or passed it in your stools. All of these symptoms, incidentally, can occur with simple ulcers. But special tests can be done to set your mind at rest.

Views on other aspects of the treatment of ulcers have changed in recent years. Prolonged bed rest is no longer thought necessary, neither is a very restricted diet. You will probably have already found out for yourself which foods seem to upset you, so it would be sensible to avoid these. In general, it is best to avoid strong coffee and tea, alcohol, cigarette smoking and all highly seasoned and spiced foods. A glass of milk and plain biscuit at bedtime can help avoid further pain during the night. Small unhurried meals at fairly frequent intervals is a good general principle to adopt.

A frequent hypochondriacal complaint concerns the bowels, usually constipation. You may be one of those people who pay far more attention than you should to your bowel function. There is a great deal to be said for leaving things to nature and giving yourself a chance to find out what your own normal bowel rhythm should be (this can vary from three times a day to once a week) rather than take laxatives. Diarrhoea, especially first thing in the morning, is often due to anxiety.

Noisy guts, passing a lot of wind, mucus or funny looking stools, may cause great concern. Some rather tense, overactive people may have tense overactive bowels which simply reflect their emotional state at the time. Worries over possible blockage, cancer or other diseases may readily occur, especially if you get depressed. Piles can be a great source of discomfort and worry and one of the possible causes for passing blood. Even today this area of the body is still regarded by some with embarrassment and shame, but don't let this deter you from seeking professional advice; your doctor won't be embarrassed.

You may have found from experience that certain items of food upset your stomach or bowels and obviously these should be avoided. There has been a lot of talk in recent years about our Western diet being responsible for a number of bowel disorders, chiefly because it is too refined and lacking in 'roughage'. This term is now out of favour and has been replaced by 'dietary fibre'. A true high-fibre diet replaces refined carbohydrates with 'whole foods' such as fruit, vegetables, pulses, nuts and wholegrain products such as 100 per cent wholewheat flour, unpolished rice and wholegrain breakfast cereals.

Such a diet promotes optimal gut function and because it's bulky and chewy, prevents excessive calorie intake. It will make the stools heavier and softer, with less need to strain at stool and also a stronger feeling of wanting to empty the bowels. There is much individual variation and a certain amount of trial and error to find what suits you is inevitable. However the simplest ways of starting are to eat wholemeal bread and wholegrain breakfast cereals. If other 'bulking' agents are going to be taken or special preparations from the chemist (as opposed to foods), medical advice should be sought first. In any case all changes should be gradually introduced.

# 5

## Fears and Phobias

When we say someone is anxious what we mean is that they feel frightened but cannot put their finger on just what it is that frightens them. It's like a feeling of dread, as if something awful is going to happen but you're not sure what. Now we have all felt like this at times, it is a universal human characteristic, but usually before something we really are dreading like going on stage, speaking in public or before an examination or interview. It is because we all have this tendency that an anxiety neurosis or state is so extremely common.

In fact a certain level of anxiety is necessary (we all have our own optimal level) as it helps to keep you alert and on your toes and for this reason has survival value. It is only when it gets out of hand, by being too intense, lasting too long or seemingly brought on by unfrightening situations or things, that you can then be said to be suffering from 'bad nerves'. You will certainly suffer and not be able to carry on as usual; in other words you're ill.

When the anxiety is focused on a particular activity, like going out shopping, or particular object like a spider, it is called a phobia or irrational fear. It is perfectly normal to have at least one mild phobia, like an animal or insect one, but usually it doesn't make much difference to your life. There are also a whole set of illness phobias or hypochondriacal fears.

When a phobia becomes an illness, as opposed to being a bit of a nuisance, is a matter of degree. If you only sometimes think about it, shall we say a fear of cancer, then it is

39

well within the bounds of normality. It is not normal when you can't stop thinking about it and it's the first thing that comes into your head when you wake up in the morning and you couldn't get to sleep anyway for worrying about it. Also if you can't concentrate properly on your job, daren't open a paper in case you should read about it or watch television for similar reasons. When it's reached this degree you usually end up in a vicious circle anyway, with worry followed by more worry.

Indeed this can take on the form of an obsession, rather like a tune running through your head, which at first is no problem, but then it keeps on coming back in spite of all efforts on your part to think of something else. Try as you might you cannot rid yourself of these repetitive, unpleasant, morbid thoughts. It's no use being told to pull yourself together, not be silly and so on, because you can't help it and certainly don't enjoy it.

There are, however, various safety devices built into our minds for coping with intolerable anxiety, particularly when it occurs in a situation in which you feel trapped and for which there seems to be no way out or easy solution. Some of these mechanisms operate below the level of the conscious mind so that they cannot be deliberately switched on or off. It was Freud who suggested that unsatisfied unconscious needs give rise either to anxiety or aggression.

One thing that sometimes happens is a kind of mental opting out. The situation is so intolerable and the anxiety so great, that you begin to feel very strange and cut off, as in a dream. It's the sort of feeling that it's not quite real, it cannot be happening to me, I must pinch myself to see if I'm really awake. This in itself can be quite alarming as you may feel rather zombie-like and at the same time may even wonder if you're going mad. You can also get strange feelings in different parts of your body, for

40

instance your head may feel bigger or smaller or your arm numb.

This sort of feeling, difficult to describe, but you'll know what I'm talking about if you've actually experienced it, is one way of trying to deal with intolerable anxiety. You can also get like this in states of extreme fatigue and after long journeys as part of 'jet-lag'. So don't be alarmed, you're not going round the bend.

Some people, by the very nature of their personality and the way they are made, are more prone than others to develop anxiety symptoms. This type is usually described as a born worrier, highly strung, very sensitive and perhaps a bit insecure and uncertain of himself. But just because you were a bit frightened of the dark as a child, shy and reluctant to go to school and anxious over exams, does not mean you are always going to be like that. We are always changing, learning and adapting.

On the other hand how you were brought up and how your natural anxiety and childish insecurity was dealt with, does play a part in how you cope later on in life. Like most other things in life you can 'learn' to be anxious and it can be 'rewarded'. For example if you felt very anxious and sick in the mornings when it was time to go to school and were then constantly kept off school because of this.

You may too have been brought up in a hypochondriacal atmosphere and there is the danger of passing this on from one generation to the next. Your health worries begin to extend to the rest of your family and do not just involve yourself.

An unfortunate experience or accidental association early in life can sometimes form the basis for a later phobia, for instance, seeing a spider just when your mother dies; the spider then becomes associated with death and feelings of panic. These early associations can be forgotten or repressed as, by and large, we tend to remember nice things and forget nasty ones, except when we get depressed and then the opposite can happen. This sort of thing can also happen later on in life when the anxiety gets displaced onto a situation which in itself is not usually a threatening one.

Many of the symptoms of anxiety are physical and are produced by a part of your nervous system over which you have little voluntary control, for instance the nerves which help to control your blood pressure and heart rate, both of which can go up when you are anxious. Modern work has shown that under certain circumstances you can in fact gain a certain amount of control over these functions in that you can be taught to 'will' your blood pressure to go higher or lower (biofeedback). This is not yet sufficiently well established to be used in treatment.

The important point is that many of the physical symptoms of anxiety can be mistaken by both doctors and you for signs of serious illness, when they are nothing of the sort. These symptoms can also become the focus for further hypochondriacal concern.

The main symptoms of anxiety are a dry mouth, feelings of sickness or actual vomiting, palpitations, a racing pulse, 'butterflies' in the stomach, trembling, sweating, a desire to pass water very often and diarrhoea. Various tension symptoms such as headache and other aches and pains have already been mentioned. You may also feel dizzy and unsteady on your feet, be generally irritable and jumpy and perhaps bite your nails, smoke, eat and drink too much.

Any of these may get picked on, let us say palpitations, when you may start to convince yourself that you've got heart disease and will soon die from a heart attack. Trembling may be socially embarrassing, so that you can't hold a cup and saucer without rattling and spilling.

You can get so nervous that you daren't go anywhere unless you are sure that there is a toilet near at hand. Excessive sweating can stain your clothes as well as cause further worry in case others notice or think you smell. This sort of sensitivity is reinforced by clever advertising; B.O. or body odour is largely a commercial invention.

If you are feeling dizzy and unsteady, you might begin to worry in case you should faint in public, draw a crowd around you and have an ambulance called; you really fear drawing attention to yourself and making a fool of yourself in public. This very rarely happens, as this type of dizziness has nothing to do with fits, epilepsy or other similar conditions.

You may get so anxious about yourself and your health that you cannot sleep. This can either be a difficulty in getting off to sleep, very light sleep with nightmares and frequent waking or feeling as if you were about to fall through the bed and suddenly jerk yourself awake. Very frightening panic attacks can occur at night, when you feel quite terrified, with a sense of constriction in the chest, a feeling you are going to choke, have a heart attack and suddenly die. Although extremely frightening these attacks are not serious.

A lot of hypochondriacal fears about insomnia are unnecessary and due to ignorance about the nature of sleep itself, and what could happen to you if you don't get enough or the right sort.

Modern research has shown that there are two types of sleep which alternate throughout the night. The first type is called paradoxical or rapid eye movement (REM for short) sleep; the other orthodox or non-rapid eye movement (NREM for short) sleep. It seems that there needs to be a minimum of about 45 minutes NREM sleep first before the appearance of the first REM sleep period of the night. The NREM phase is further subdivided into four stages.

The majority of stages three and four (deepest sleep) occur in the first half of the night, while REM sleep is dominant in the second half of the night.

REM sleep is so named because at this stage your eyes move about in a series of jerks as if you were scanning a scene or watching your own dreams. In fact, most of our dreams occur only during this stage of sleep. Also during REM sleep penile erections occur, blood pressure increases, so does the heart rate, with a state very like one of general excitement. Normally each phase of REM sleep lasts about 20–30 minutes and is longer the later in the night it occurs.

There seems to be a particular need for REM sleep and its accompanying dreams. This phase of sleep may also have important connections with learning and memory and for laying down proteins in our tissues. This could be reflected in the fact that in adults the proportion of the night spent in REM sleep is about 25 per cent, whereas in babies it is about 50 per cent.

There is also a need for stages three and four of NREM sleep, as during these stages there is increased activity in the blood forming organs as well as increased output of growth hormone. Note that growth hormone in adults is not for growth; it helps to build up protein tissue and break down fat deposits to produce energy. So that very roughly, we could say that REM sleep is concerned with brain repair and NREM sleep with body repair. But it does not follow that missing some will either send you mad or make you a physical wreck!

However, one recent finding, not yet generally accepted, suggested that disturbance of stage four NREM sleep could be an important factor in some cases of 'fibrositis'. It was in those who showed morning aching and stiffness, which was temporarily improved by heat, and seemingly affected by the weather, accompanied by sleep disturbance, poor appetite and chronic fatigue. It was not just a case of pain preventing you going into a deep sleep, but rather the other way round, ending, presumably in a vicious circle.

It does seem to be true that different people need different amounts of sleep, just like some people seem able to take short 'cat naps' during the day and feel refreshed afterwards. But this is not a firmly fixed characteristic as your sleep requirements vary with age, general health, what you've been doing during the daytime, how much you've had to eat and drink and so on.

Many brain workers and worrying types often do experience some difficulty in getting off to sleep while other very active types tend to wake early and like to get on with things. But do remember that a few sleepless nights, of whatever sort, won't hurt you, as you can catch up later, and Nature tends to redress the balance for you. We are pretty adaptable really, and going on night-shift or to the other side of the world will obviously take a bit of getting used to at first, but you will soon get into new habits.

Don't go flying to the sleeping pills, or even worse, start taking aspirins, as these only work if it's pain that's keeping you awake. Alcohol, most sleeping pills and some tranquillizers have a very selective effect on your sleep in that initially they decrease the proportion of time you spend in REM sleep. But with continued administration, this effect wears off. When the drugs are stopped there is frequently a rebound effect, as if you have to make up for all the 'lost' REM sleep and its accompanying dreams, with consequent restlessness, 'bad' nights and nightmares. This can go on for days, and sometimes even for weeks, so don't mistake it as a sign for going back on pills again, or even increasing the dose! Beware of advertisements which promise you 'natural' sleep with unnatural drugs.

Instead try to understand why you are suffering from insomnia at this particular time—there may be a simple reason. Occasionally difficulty in falling asleep points to an anxiety state or waking up very early to depression, which require treatment in their own right. For ordinary insomnia, try to cultivate the art of both mental and physical relaxation. Don't start getting worked up hours before bedtime and convince yourself that you will never sleep tonight or get into a habit of thinking you always have a bad night on certain nights, for example, Sundays.

Try other simple methods before seeing your doctor or resorting to drugs. Go to bed later, have a warm (not too hot) bath, try an evening stroll, a warm drink (not tea or coffee) at bedtime. Read something light or amusing and try to think of something pleasant when falling asleep. A good orgasm can also be helpful in relaxing you. In any case, you often sleep far better and for much longer than you realize.

Because you always feel tired, seem to have no energy and awake unrefreshed, don't always assume that it's all due to lack of sleep. 'Living on your nerves' can literally use up a lot of your energy. You may also find you've got more emotional than usual. A sad play on T.V. or something you read in the papers suddenly causes you to burst into tears. It's also quite common to feel depressed as well, particularly if you've been anxious for rather a long time. This can then come over you in waves and you find yourself very up and down, with good days and bad ones.

You can also get very sensitive to noise, which will not be helped if you happen to live near a busy airport or main road or if you share your house with a teenager who likes loud music. Other 'noises' may be experienced in your head or ears; sometimes what you are really hearing, especially when quiet at night, is your own pulse beating.

We have already mentioned how common some phobias are, especially very mild ones. One big disease phobia which still tops the list, is fear of cancer. How many of us when suffering from some quite minor illness haven't for a moment wondered if it wasn't something 'more serious'. Cancer has become a dread word and to actually have it almost socially embarrassing.

Strictly speaking there is no such thing as cancer, only growths and tumours of different tissues and organs of the body, which vary from the completely harmless to the very malignant with a tendency to spread. There are many grades in between these two extremes. But in any case, particularly when tackled early, modern methods of treatment are proving more and more successful. Fears of mutilating operations may add to your anxiety and cause further delay in seeking help.

A cancer phobia can be made worse by knowing it's in the family or by hearing of the death of a close friend or someone dear to you. Although basically it's a good thing to bring the subject out into the open, discuss it, and put the facts before the public, there is a danger of overdoing it. We hear so much nowadays about examining your own breasts, cervical smears, smoking and all sorts of 'scares' from the birth pill to hair sprays and various items of diet, that it's tempting to ignore the lot. You then end up saying something like, you've got to die from something, so what the hell, let's carry on as usual, a short life and a merry one.

Fears of death itself are pretty universal although you may confuse fears of dying with fears of death. The former is much more common, like a fear of dying in pain (which should never happen now) or even of being buried alive. This again has been reinforced by publicity and discussion about the 'moment of death' and when exactly you do die, especially when kept going on a machine. Talk of organ and tissue transplants may also add to your morbid thoughts. Death itself may be feared for its utter finality, futility and nothingness; this is when a strong religious faith can be very helpful.

Other allied fears are of old age, being helpless and a burden to others, or 'going like' grandma or auntie, or some other relative. Very few conditions are directly inherited, and so, for example, just because someone in your family had Parkinson's disease, it doesn't necessarily follow that you're bound to get it as well. If you are really worried by this sort of thing, ask your doctor, and if he's unsure there are now a number of specialist centres available for genetic counselling.

Another common fear is of going mad. The usual idea of this is of something going snap in your head, having a 'brainstorm', and going berserk and doing all sorts of violent things without really realizing what you are doing. Madness just does not happen in this way. An anxiety neurosis and panic attacks have nothing to do with madness or serious mental illness.

We hear a lot these days about baby batterers but the sort of person who does indulge in this sort of violence is very different from the anxious and depressed mother who fears she might harm her baby. Thoughts of harming their baby have passed through the minds of most mothers particularly after several sleepless nights due to baby's constant crying. But again, to actually indulge in any physical violence is extremely rare. Similarly if you get into an emotional state following childbirth, thoughts and fears are not usually carried out in actions.

Lesser fears of doctors, hospitals and dentists are understandable but most of us manage to overcome them, usually from experience, as it is nearly always the thinking about it beforehand—anticipatory anxiety—which is so much worse than the actual experience itself.

Another sort of phobia involves fear of travelling on your own. For instance any of the symptoms of anxiety can occur when flying or travelling on a bus or out shopping. This may reach the stage of your becoming housebound and then even of being frightened while on your own in the house, so your husband has to have time off work to be with you. The fear is essentially of situations over which you have not got full control, so that travelling in your own car, at least initially, is possible, for then you can stop and get out when you want and not cause any fuss, a thing you can't do on public transport. Similarly getting stuck in a queue to pay to get out of a supermarket can throw you into a panic; you feel trapped and don't know what to do.

An allied situation occurs with some social functions, such as eating in public, when you may feel sick and faint and unable to swallow your food for fear of choking, so that eating in the office canteen or going out to dinner can become sheer torture. This can well cause further guilt and embarrassment, as it is a difficult thing to explain to others.

All this can undermine your self-confidence and make you feel very inferior and inadequate. Or you may become 'tongue-tied' in company, not knowing what to say, getting all hot and bothered into the bargain, and finding yourself quite unable to indulge in any sort of small talk. Very anxious people tend to go to one extreme or the other of either clamming up altogether or talking too much and too quickly. If you do have these difficulties in expressing yourself, try instead to be a good listener, as this is often very much appreciated by others.

# 6

## Highly Hysterical

Yet another type of hypochondriac is the hysterical, the traditional female variety. The history of the use of the term hysteria is very interesting and has much in common with that already outlined for hypochondria. This may also be a very early example of male chauvinism.

The word is derived from the Greek and means womb or uterus, so right from the start it was associated with women and sex. Hysterectomy, the operation for the removal of the womb has the same derivation. The ancient theory was that the womb was rather like an animal which got restless and moved about the body and in so doing caused various symptoms. Later on the womb was actually referred to as 'the mother' and we then had the rather fancy name for choking sensations and a feeling of a lump in the throat as 'the suffocation of the mother'!

Of course this theory, made up by male doctors and others, is not true, but the name persists to this day and so do some of the old ideas. When hysterical symptoms were first described in men, this was ridiculed as a preposterous idea; how could a man suffer from hysteria when he didn't have a womb?

But again, like hypochondria, hysteria has acquired many meanings over the years, including meaning the same as hypochondriasis only in women. So that by tradition similar symptoms may get these different labels by reason only of the sex of the patient and perhaps the sex of the doctor too!

The popular idea of the hysteric is still a young woman uncontrollably crying and laughing and who responds best to a sharp slap on the face or a douche of cold water.

Closely allied to this is the so-called hysterical personality. You will note that the characteristics which feature in this personality type are all rather unflattering ones, often made by males about women.

The characteristics are vanity, attention-seeking, extreme moodiness, emotional shallowness, sexually provocative yet frigid, immature, easily swayed and resentfully dependent. If it is going to be used at all perhaps a better name would be a histrionic personality rather than hysterical. But the point is we are not talking about symptoms but a pattern of behaviour habitually shown by somebody as part of their life style.

The trouble is once you get this sort of label attached to you there is a tendency for others not to take your complaints so seriously; she's only acting or being childish again and wants to be in the limelight. Even though it may look rather theatrical, exaggerated and naive the suffering and pain lying behind it can be very real indeed.

Another facet of the hysterical type is to be very 'suggestible', that is to be swayed by every breeze, and to show a habitual readiness to react to others' ideas. So that other people's symptoms may be copied or 'caught', and doctors have to be very careful not to keep asking about all sorts of symptoms in case of putting ideas into your head which you then take up.

Actual hysterical symptoms of a physical kind are called conversion symptoms which means that inner conflicts and anxieties are converted into physical symptoms. How the mysterious leap from mind to body is brought about is another matter but it certainly can happen. The symptoms produced are not a matter of chance or coincidence, for they directly express, in a hidden way (symbolize), what the inner conflict is all about and at the same time offer a temporary solution.

Chest pain may be due to unexpressed hostility or guilt;

after all we say you want to get something off your chest or make a clean breast of it. This may also symbolize rejection, being heartless or broken hearted. Paralysis of an arm might mean you would really like to clobber somebody but you're afraid of the consequences. This is not a deliberate conscious act which is put on.

But if you are of the personality type just described, to some outside observers the seemingly exaggerated and dramatic ways in which you present your symptoms can lead to difficulties particularly if there appears to be a discrepancy in that you don't appear to be suffering as you say you are. You may even be feeling quite desperate and depressed but can only express this in your own habitual way. This also applies to anxiety symptoms.

On the other hand because of easy suggestibility and some of the other difficulties already mentioned, you may go on accumulating various symptoms, until you end up with a multitude of complaints. Not only that but the whole pattern of these symptoms does not fit into that of any conventional physical illness described in a textbook of medicine.

Another set of hysterical symptoms is concerned with psychological rather than physical ways of dealing with intractable problems and conflicts. This involves a psychological separation or splitting off, so that the unpleasant ideas are banished from the mind. This is based on the normal tendency to remember nice things and forget nasty ones. However in hysterical states this tendency is grossly exaggerated and goes too far, so that you may end up with no memory at all or a big gap in your memory. This is sometimes associated with wandering off in an apparently confused state and not being able to remember who you are or what you should be doing. In this way you can defer or postpone experiencing the emotional impact, which can even be a severe depression with suicidal ideas.

Because of the tendency to be easily influenced you can understand how minor epidemics of hysterical behaviour can occur, especially under certain circumstances, like living very closely together, as in a convent or school. Indeed a modern example of this occurred in a girls' Comprehensive school in a class of 16–17 year olds who were shortly taking examinations. They started to fall down in a sort of faint, and at one time no fewer than eight girls and a young locum teacher lay apparently unconscious on the floor.

Because of the many different forms and ways of using the term hysteria, exactly as with hypochondria, it will come as no surprise for you to learn that if you took a group of patients all diagnosed as suffering from 'hysteria', you would find a very motley collection of people. This has been done, more than once, and not only have the groups been very thoroughly studied at the time, they have also been followed up over a number of years to see what happens to them.

Results show little in the way of direct inheritance and surprisingly, there were not a great number of hysterical personalities, although there was a bias towards immature females. Anxiety and depression were quite commonly found. Overall there seemed to be two broad groupings. One with a sudden onset of symptoms who got better quickly and another who had more disturbed personalities and lives with multiple symptoms which fluctuated but never got entirely better.

A similar type of patient was recently described by doctors specializing in the treatment of rheumatic conditions as—

one who never improves whatever treatment is given and whose diagnosis always remains uncertain ... they crave medical and surgical (but not psychiatric) attention to make them legitimately ill persons. They are specialists in their own illness and symptomatology. They soon exhaust their friends, relatives and doctors by the unaltered chronicity of their complaints and their constant full-time dedication to them ...

This also illustrates the frustration sometimes felt by doctors in trying to help such patients.

In one follow-up study of a group of hysterics, years later, over half did in fact develop a significant physical illness. The point is you can react hysterically to an already established physical illness or behave like this even before the underlying physical illness has become obvious. So doctors have to be very careful in making a diagnosis of either hysteria or hypochondria.

Again I would like to emphasize that hysterics are not a race apart and like any other neurotic condition, hysterical reactions are firmly based in normality and are a potential we all possess. One big difficulty which always arises with hysterical conditions is, are you putting it on, pretending just to gain attention, to get your own way or to get your own back, rather like a child. In many cases (as in conversion symptoms) a lot goes on at an unconscious level, so that you don't fully realize yourself what is going on at the back of your mind. It may be a 'gain' in the sense that, at least temporarily, it gives you peace of mind, but it is not something that can be switched on and off at will.

There is no denying, though, that illness can be a handy way of avoiding making important decisions or of getting out of difficult situations. But actual frank downright malingering, deliberately and consciously pretending you are ill when you jolly well know you aren't, is very rare. Some would go so far as to say that if you are reduced to behaving in this way, then you must be sick anyway!

There are indeed certain very rare individuals who do go around the country, using assumed names, 'collapsing' near hospitals and pretending they are ill. They can be experts in mimicking certain diseases and get up to all sorts of tricks to try and deceive doctors. They may actually enjoy being operated on or else they want to be given certain drugs.

There are some borderline cases. For instance after an industrial accident, say involving a head injury, compensation proceedings may drag on for years, involving many different examinations and reports by many different doctors. Obviously to suddenly get well and lose all your symptoms would also lose you your chances of getting any compensation, which after a certain period of time you think you very much deserve. After all you've had to put up with a lot of pain and disability.

It seems that hysterical reactions are decreasing but it is in this area that fashions have such an influence, both in what sorts of symptoms are produced and how they are treated. I have already said something about the 'sick role' and how you can look at these things from the point of view of why you behave like this. Extending this approach a little further you will be able to see possible connections between this way of looking at things and why the young, the immature and women are especially vulnerable.

The young have only recently stopped being children and the immature are still children at heart, so it is easier for them to slip back again into a state like childhood dependency, which is what happens when you are ill. You then, once again, become dependent on others, are cared for, have no responsibilities and get extra love and affection.

Women are still, by and large, dependent on men, discriminated against and find it difficult to reach positions of power and authority. So that they may be forced into manipulative and devious modes of behaviour, both to try and achieve power and at the same time to express their disgust and hostility. Here we have the 'tease', the young attractive woman who tries to gain power by using sexual allure; she eggs men on but then refuses to deliver the goods. She will then complain that men only want one thing. Basically she really hates them, wishes to humiliate them, and show them up as weak and rotten. In fact such women make good short-term flirts but disastrous wives and mothers. They have often been spoilt as little girls by a weak over-indulgent father. But this sort of behaviour is nonetheless partly condoned by men (including male doctors) if the woman is attractive, when she may be given the benefit of the doubt, considered really to be ill (hysterical) and taken on for treatment.

There are several possible reasons why gross hysterical conversion symptoms are now rare; more equality and Women's Lib plus better all round education and understanding generally. This does not mean they have entirely disappeared. They can still occur in those of modest intellectual endowment, in those from different cultures and in anybody in a situation of extreme stress such as war time. What has also happened is that with better education, symptoms have become more subtle and sophisticated. Instead of getting total paralysis of both legs because you are having difficulties in 'standing on your own two feet' the complaints now may be of dizzy spells, or being frustrated, unfulfilled or alienated.

# 7

# How Depressing

Many hypochondriacs are suffering from a form of depressive illness which can go unrecognized for long periods because all the presenting complaints are physical. Also people tend to assume that if you are suffering from depression you should be crying a lot and the whole thing should be obvious. This is not the case as it is often very difficult to cry when you are severely depressed, even though you may feel like it.

The trouble is that different people mean different things by 'depression'. Doctors realize this and will be on the look out for other symptoms of depression when patients come along and ask for a tonic, say they feel rundown or have no energy. The same can happen with hypochondriacal complaints such as constant worry over constipation or 'nervous dyspepsia'.

By depression I mean a feeling of sadness and despair, perhaps better described as feelings of hopelessness and helplessness, which have some features in common with ordinary sadness and grief. The more severe type of depression is basically a physical illness itself. But we needn't enter into the endless professional debates as to how many different types of depression there are and whether they are quite separate illnesses or simply more or less severe forms of the same thing. Depression can also occur as a reaction to having a severe illness or disability of any sort. Indeed depression can itself be a symptom of another illness.

We all get moody at times, the 'Monday morning blues', feeling 'browned off', 'fed-up' and so on. There is a special part of the brain which is concerned with controlling our moods and this can get out of order or seem to be 'set' rather too high or low in some individuals. Important hormones (chemical messengers) and other chemical constituents of the blood and brain are involved as well. Although depression does tend to run in families, it is not inherited as such, only the tendency to react in this way.

Some people are by nature mood swingers and have a more than average tendency to develop depression or its opposite (mania). But other types are also vulnerable in this respect, for instance the very anxious, fussy and conscientious types. Anxiety and depression often occur together, as already outlined in Chapter 5.

When we do get depressed it alters our whole outlook on life, past, present and future. It clouds our judgement and estimation of our own worth. This is why it's important not to make big decisions (e.g. give up your job, make a new will, move house or run away) while you are still in a depressed state. In any event you will probably find it difficult to make decisions of any sort, as both mind and body are often slowed up.

This slowing up can actually affect your digestive tract as well, so that you may get a bad taste in the mouth, food tastes different or tasteless, you lose your appetite and become constipated. All sorts of bodily sensations, previously unnoticed, now come to your attention.

Many of the symptoms of depression and indeed some of the causes as well can be understood in terms of various 'losses'. For instance you can lose your appetite, weight, sleep, energy, and sense of humour, religious faith, will to live and efficiency. You begin to run yourself down, feel a failure, that you lack will power and guts, and have let everybody down. The future looks bleak and you may even think about suicide.

You may not realize that most people, at some time in their lives, have thought about suicide. It is not such a dreadful and wicked thing to think (and not now considered a crime, although to make a suicide pact or incite somebody to do it, still is) particularly when it's the result of an illness, and depression is very definitely an illness. Don't keep this as a guilty secret, share it with somebody else and you'll be surprised how understanding others can be.

Some other physical symptoms of depression, apart from generally feeling ill, are feelings of pressure in the head or chest, heaviness of the limbs, indigestion and aches and pains of all sorts. It's no wonder you get hypochondriacal. Phobias easily develop—of going mad, or having cancer, that your inside is all wrong, your bowels are blocked up and such like. These can turn from fears that you *might* have these things to firm convictions (delusions) that you actually have them and nothing will convince you to the contrary.

Because of your low self-esteem and low mood you may feel terribly guilty and wicked. You may even think of some very trivial thing you've done in the past which now begins to assume the proportions of a major crime or sin. You can feel damned and in need of punishment or that people know about these things and are talking about you in a nasty way.

You can get so miserable that you don't know what to do with yourself; you pace about all day, unable to concentrate on anything, with a poor memory for recent events. You can even begin to look older, with a sluggish circulation and a dry skin. In women the monthly periods may stop, become irregular or heavier.

Depression can occur at any age but will show in rather different ways. In the very young it may come out as bad or irresponsible behaviour. The older you get the more likely it is to present with physical symptoms and hypo-chondriacal complaints.

When mixed up with other neurotic reactions, like an anxiety neurosis, or when the depression is an obvious reaction to a big shock, the symptoms tend to fluctuate. And with this sort of depression you do tend to cry a lot and rather than blame yourself tend to blame others or 'fate', bad luck or unfortunate circumstances. Appetite and weight may actually increase as some people tend to eat more to comfort themselves, as well as drink or smoke too much as well. Sleep will also be disturbed. Headaches and all sorts of hypochondriacal fears are common.

Depression may come on especially if you are liable to react like this anyway, under special circumstances. In men after retirement, when unemployed or even some-times after promotion. In women as part of premenstrual tension (usually during the week before the period is due) following childbirth or abortion, or with some types of contraceptive pill. In either sex depression can follow a virus infection, like influenza or glandular fever. De-pression may also occur after an operation such as a hysterectomy.

One of the commonest sorts of loss that most of us have to face at some time or other in our lives is the death of a loved one. To express grief during bereavement is normal enough but sometimes this gets out of hand and becomes morbid. In a normal grief reaction a preoccupation with memories of the deceased person, including vivid dreams of him, occur. Along with this you may actually imagine, 'hear' or 'see' him, and feel his very presence.

Some of the symptoms of depression already men-tioned may occur, often coming over you in waves. This can also happen with various physical symptoms such as a choking sensation, shortness of breath, tightness in the throat or an empty feeling inside. Rheumaticky aches and pains, and in fact pretty well any of the hypochondriacal symptoms mentioned in this book, can also occur. Withdrawal from social contact, restlessness and behaviour aimed at keeping alive memories of the deceased will also occur, as well as very mixed-up feelings of anger and resentment.

Abnormal or morbid grief reactions occur almost exclusively in women. Imagine the situation of the woman who has devoted the best years of her life to nursing her ageing invalid mother, who finally dies after a long and difficult-to-bear illness. Her daughter may have now missed all chances of getting married, whilst all other members of the family have 'escaped' and made their own lives. She may have had a very strong sense of duty and been the only one in the family able to cope with a difficult, demanding and ungrateful mother. How mixed up she must feel when her mother eventually dies.

If she was, too, the sort of person who usually bottles up her feelings, then what can happen is there is no immediate expression of grief either at the time of the death or at the funeral. She may even be congratulated for being 'so brave' and for coping so well. But it has all been boiling up inside her and must find expression sooner or later. These 'delayed reactions' can be quite severe.

Other ways in which morbid grief differs from normal are in its intensity, and going on for too long, over six months or even for years. Of the many possible symptoms, great difficulties in actually accepting the loss, guilt feelings, acute anxiety attacks and suicidal ideas are prominent. The hypochondriacal symptoms experienced at this time may be very similar to those symptoms suffered by the deceased person during his last illness.

Whatever form your hypochondriacal depression takes there are several good things to remember. Depression by and large has a good outlook as there is a strong tendency built in by Nature for it to get better anyway, as long as you don't do anything silly in the meantime. Also you will get completely back to normal again; there are no lasting effects on your brain, or on your mental or physical efficiency. Finally modern methods of treatment are extremely effective both in shortening an attack of depression and in helping to stop it happening again.

A lot of this you will simply have to take 'on trust' as it is difficult to see any hope at all while you're still in a depression. And even if you may not think very highly of yourself, depression is a perfectly 'respectable' illness. You would not be blaming yourself if you'd got pneumonia for instance. Just having a change or taking a holiday may not work, in fact if you are very depressed it can make you feel even worse, so you may well need a bit of expert help.

# 8

## Out of Mind

There is a group of mental disorders, that often start in adolescence or early youth, which may initially look very similar to one of the neurotic reactions already described. Or they may appear to be just an exaggeration of adolescent problems, including worries over appearance and health. But gradually other symptoms develop, such as difficulties in thinking and expressing yourself, strange moods, and your imagination playing tricks on you so that you get hold of the wrong end of the stick and believe people are getting at you, when they're not.

This sort of development, a kind of 'persecution complex', is not really as abnormal as it sounds. It is based on a tendency we all possess, to recognize our own faults in others rather than in ourselves. Also it is easy to imagine when you walk into a room full of people and they stop talking, that they were talking about you. Or that people in a restaurant all stare at you. These types of reaction are more likely to occur if there is something you are feeling a bit guilty about.

Similarly with feelings of jealousy. You can make yourself quite ill over doubts about somebody you love yet can't really trust; again it might well be that you don't really trust yourself.

Schizophrenia is popularly known as 'split mind' but it is not a Jekyll-Hyde sort of split. Outside fiction this sort of double or multiple personality occurs in a person with marked hysterical traits and is probably artificially produced by the expectations of over-enthusiastic doctors investigating the case. In schizophrenia mental functions

63

become fragmented in that ideas and their appropriate emotions may get separated and wrongly attached to each other, so that the idea that you have cancer is accompanied by laughter and behaviour of a silly and quite inappropriate kind.

Peculiar feelings may occur in any part of your body or you may feel utterly perplexed and that you are losing your grip on reality. Thoughts, feelings and actions appear to be not your own so that you feel like a puppet with someone outside you pulling the strings. Vague hypochondriacal ideas occur but are accompanied by a callous indifference rather than anxiety or depression. Interest is lost and long periods may be spent in bed or aimlessly drifting about in a dreamy state. Early promise, shown in good school work and reports, is not fulfilled, and any sort of warm contact with others is lost.

Hypochondriacal ideas may be fostered by popular literature so that masturbation or the monthly periods are blamed for causing all the symptoms. Diffuse philosophical ideas may be entertained and because the feelings are so strange or frightening, explanations or relief may be sought in various cults or semi-mystical religious movements. Also little understood scientific advances can be blamed, like too much radiation, X-rays or wireless signals, actually playing on your body and causing symptoms.

What started out as mere preoccupations or fears about illness now become certainties. No amount of reassurance, examination or special tests will convince you otherwise. You feel suspicious that you are not being told the whole truth, so that in the face of all the evidence to the contrary, you retain a firmly fixed belief (delusion) that you have the disease.

Also hypochondriacal delusions can take both a bizarre and very literal or concrete form. For example your heart has turned to stone so that you daren't go in water in case you sink and drown or that there is an animal inside you causing a lot of noisy movement.

In other cases misinterpretations turn into firmly established facts; the noises and flashes of light during the night was not just a passing motorist but a deliberate attempt by nasty neighbours to keep you awake, annoy you and make you ill. Other experiences like hearing someone speak to you when you can't see anybody around (hallucinations) can also occur.

Similar experiences can follow taking illicit drugs such as 'pep pills' and 'speed' (amphetamine and methedrine) or a 'bad trip' on 'acid' (LSD) or indeed from alcohol abuse with D.T.s (delirium tremens) or the 'horrors'. This is one reason why a lot of people regard schizophrenia as a physical illness with some chemical upset affecting the brain. Chronic abuse of these drugs, including alcohol, may well eventually produce permanent brain damage and other physical changes; but in the early stages hypochondriacal fears and delusions can be prominent symptoms.

The alcoholic can damage not only his liver, heart, stomach and nervous system but also get depressed, guilty and preoccupied with his health. It's like having a permanent hangover but not being able to stop drinking or always indulging in the 'hair of the dog'. Of course you may have started drinking in the first place because you felt anxious, depressed, insecure or lonely.

In older age groups brain damage may result from changes in the blood supply to the brain, sometimes associated with longstanding high blood pressure. A condition of dementia results. Again 'demented' is a term in popular use but in its strict medical sense it means deterioration of intellectual functions due to some physical disease or injury to the brain.

There is a tendency anyway, with increasing age, to

think more about yourself and your health. Increasing loneliness, as your friends and relatives die, with perhaps failing eyesight and hearing and gradual loss of independence, can all help to cause depression and hypochondriacal worries.

The very old who go 'soft in the head' or 'senile' (demented) are mostly women for the simple reason that on average women outlive men by several years. The younger ones with changes in their blood vessels are more commonly men.

A 'difficult' and demanding granny can be a trial all round. If she keeps on telling you the same things over and over again, gets confused and forgetful, wanders about at night and sleeps during the day, she is likely to be suffering from dementia. Repetitive hypochondriacal complaints are common, such as headaches, giddiness, noises in the ears and feelings of discomfort in the chest. Minor strokes can also occur.

The condition can fluctuate and be very distressing for the old person concerned. She can be very well aware that she is 'breaking up' and may pathetically complain that she can't help it; crying and shouting may be rapidly followed by laughing. This self-awareness can produce a state of depression, which in turn brings further hypochondriacal self-scrutiny. Sometimes a severe depression can mimic dementia or the two can go hand in hand. The depression will respond very much better to treatment and although a lot can be done to help the elderly demented, the dementia itself cannot be cured as lost brain cells are not replaced.

But do not get the idea that dementia is inevitable, it isn't, and many old people keep all their faculties right up to the end. Old age has many positive features and should not be dreaded. Much, however, depends on society's attitudes.

# 9

## Out of Character

When we say somebody acted 'out of character', we mean unlike his normal self. Here we are concerned with that normal self or personality in all its vagaries, as this is crucial for a proper understanding of why you become ill when you do and why it takes this particular form. We will also see the effect different personality types, both normal and abnormal, can have on the development of hypochondriacal symptoms.

The name 'personality' comes from the Latin ('Persona') meaning a mask, which actors used to wear in classical plays to show to the audience what sort of characters they were portraying. In other words we show what we are really like in social situations, in reacting with or indeed in avoiding, other people. It determines our life style or how we habitually feel, think and behave.

As we are all a bit different from each other it is naturally very difficult to make a classification which would include every possible type of personality. There is also the problem of how and what to measure. The best way of thinking about it is to visualize personality as being made up of a mixture of traits or characteristics, some of which can be measured and some not but many of which are exact opposites of each other. An example would be the famous division into extraverts and introverts.

The extravert is a more outgoing sort who dislikes being on his own, loves company, is seldom shy or short of something to say. By contrast the introvert tends to be quieter, more solitary, not so boisterous and happy on his own. These are normal variations, although in our society (as opposed to the East) the extravert is regarded (wrongly) as being the more normal and healthy. Actually most of us are a mixture and this could be said about all sorts of other traits such as dependent-independent, passive-aggressive and so on.

The reasons we are as we are depend on both heredity and how we were brought up as well as other early influences in our lives. We also change as we grow older, 'life begins at forty' can mean, amongst other things, that by this age some people become more relaxed, outgoing and more sure of themselves.

There is also a physical aspect to personality, sometimes covered by the term constitution ('he has the constitution of an ox') or general make-up. An important aspect of this is the sort of nervous system you have, whether it is very reactive or not. There is some tie up as well between physique and personality. Examples are the fat, jolly extravert, and the taller, thinner, introvert.

The temperament or feeling part of you determines whether you come across as a very warm sort of person or seem a bit aloof and distant, whether you 'wear your heart on your sleeve' or keep your feelings to yourself, whether you are a worrier or pretty carefree.

Finally your whole way of life is very much determined by your personality and hence indirectly your health, particularly by reason of certain habits. Obvious examples here are smoking, the amount you eat and whether you have a tendency to run to fat or not, drinking, drug taking and amount of exercise you take.

When one or more character traits are grossly exaggerated the personality becomes lop-sided in its development and we can then speak of a personality disorder. Some of these have already been mentioned: the hysterical (Chapter 6) and the anxious (Chapter 5).

What about the hypochondriacal personality type and

the various forms this can take? Again we are mostly dealing with exaggerations of normal concern over health and
appearance, not symptoms, but habits of a lifetime. Such
behaviour as over-indulgence in patent medicines, food
fads, frequent visits to the doctor with vague or trivial
complaints just to 'make sure'. Perhaps an extreme
interest in keep fit and physical culture, a preoccupation
with bowel function and constant reference to medical
dictionaries and books. An inability to go anywhere
without a large medicine chest. Morning rituals of looking
at your tongue, eyes, feeling your pulse or taking some
'cleansing' preparation.

A common denominator to all this could be concern
over avoiding disease rather than a fear of having one.
Nonetheless there may be much talk of illness and a
great willingness to swap medical and surgical histories
with anyone interested enough to participate.

Another personality type particularly prone to hypochondriacal worries is the obsessional. Again we are
speaking of an extreme or exaggerated type, as it is a very
good thing to have some obsessional traits in your personality as this will make you punctual, reliable and
conscientious. If, however, you have too many you can
end up being so conscientious that everybody takes you
for granted and you are in danger of becoming a doormat
and afraid to say 'no'. You will also find it hard to relax,
you will hate 'wasting time' and you may develop such an
outsize conscience that you feel guilty at the drop of a hat.
You can turn into a fussy perfectionist; everything must
be just so, everything in its place and a place for everything. The houseproud housewife who says 'you can eat
your dinner off my kitchen floor' is another example.

Unfortunately the extremely obsessional type is very
prone to doubts, will double check everything, and deep
down may even doubt himself. With this goes a 'thing'

about cleanliness, germs, dirt and hygiene. There is also a fear of change, novelty and the unknown. If you are also prone to get tense and anxious, as is often the case, then tension symptoms like neckache and headaches are easily produced.

At some time you will have to 'give in' and have time off work but no doubt will still see this as a sign of weakness. You may also have a fear of getting hooked on pills, so that you would rather suffer than take something. In fact you often fear any situation over which you have not got full control such as getting drunk or having an anaesthetic.

We must distinguish here, and this applies to all the personality types, between traits and symptoms. Obsessionals provide a good example. An obsession (symptom) is an idea, like a phobia, which gets into your mind, which you recognize as silly but try as you might you cannot get rid of it. There is a battle within yourself to try and stop thinking morbid thoughts, but they tend to recur with a big build-up of tension and anxiety, with only temporary relief by giving in. Such ruminations may concern your health, diet, fears of contamination or violence.

A compulsion is a similar tendency to do something, rather than think or worry about it, like washing your hands again and again or for a certain number of times. This may start by washing your hands twice after going to the toilet or after touching a door handle, just in case the first time wasn't thorough enough. Behaviour rather like this is found in children's games: having to touch every other lamp-post or not tread on every third crack in the pavement otherwise some disaster will befall you. Adult superstitions may make you throw the spilt salt, rather shamefacedly, over your left shoulder just in case, although you know it's silly.

Another personality disorder which in many respects is

almost the exact opposite of the obsessional, is called psychopathic. This type couldn't care less about anyone or anything, with seemingly no conscience at all. It's an 'I'm all right Jack' approach to life, with an inability to learn from experience or appreciate the feelings of others. This may go with a tendency to extreme irritability and explosive outbursts of rage. There is often a history of a lifelong battle with authority, starting with difficulties at home (although frequently coming from an emotionally deprived background) and school, in holding down a job and getting on with people generally. Here new sensations and situations are constantly sought, things are done just for 'kicks'.

Over-indulgence in alcohol and drugs, as well as sexual promiscuity, are further attributes. If the person concerned is abnormally aggressive, as opposed to seriously inadequate, it is usually others that do the complaining. But curiously some of these types when met again many years later have developed into hypochondriacs, often with an outsize chip on the shoulder as well.

A further variety is the person who is always clinging to others, never seems to be able to cope on his own, has never been robust and may have been a weakly child. They seem to have low reserves of energy, and lack drive and initiative. Such types may suffer from 'nervous debility' and can spend a lot of time off work.

An excessive degree of introversion produces the shy, dreamy loner, who shuns contact with other people. He appears distant and cold but can suffer a lot inwardly. Another type is the reserved suspicious one, who can never accept anything at face value and always feels there must be a catch in it somewhere. They tend to get quarrelsome and put people's backs up and may even feel that everybody is against them. They may so distrust doctors that they insist on second opinions and are never satisfied, even to the extent, on occasions, of going to court and indulging in protracted litigation.

Then there are the professional martyrs, who love to suffer and take on everybody else's troubles. They may even like being 'guinea pigs' and volunteer only too readily for experiments. They may have a pressing need to prove themselves.

The combinations and variations are endless, but the main points are that how we see ourselves, what sort of lives we lead, our beliefs, attitudes and habits, are all important factors in determining how we face up to both illness and the fear of illness. The middle-aged man with a markedly obsessional personality who is constantly fussing over his health and has been for many years, is the sort of person who is sometimes said to suffer from hypochondria, as if this was a specific disease in its own right and which was not understandable in any other way.

I think it's much better to try and understand hypochondriacal symptoms in all the other ways described in this book.

# 10

## Sexual Hangups

No section on sexual problems would be complete without a reference to Freud. His reputation for putting everything down to sex is not really fair or accurate. He used the word 'sexual' in a much wider sense than just genital, implying pleasure derived from various bodily zones. On hypochondria in general his original theory was that it resulted from the toxic effects of damned-up libido (the energy of the love instincts). It was therefore a physical condition so would not be amenable to psychological analysis. Perhaps the nearest modern equivalent would be to say that sexual frustration or being sex starved was a possible factor.

We are supposed to be living in a 'permissive society' where anything goes and doing what comes naturally is the order of the day. For all this there is still a great deal of ignorance about sexual matters and if anything, sexual problems seem to be more frequent than ever. Just what constitutes sexual health and happiness is not always easy to say.

In many ways there is too much talk about it, with the commercial exploitation and cheapening of sex. To some, efforts at sex education are self-defeating and are simply providing more stimulating and titillating pictures and literature. There is also the danger that 'sex manuals' increase rather than decrease feelings of sexual inadequacy. It is also the only form of education where 'practicals' are discouraged.

But if it is all left to parents or for the young to find out for themselves, what happens? I recall one young patient telling me what her mother had told her about monthly periods—'if you don't lose you'll go daft'—that's all. Another received her sole sex education from her father with the following—'keep your knees together until you get married'.

We get the types of neurosis we deserve. There is still a hopeless muddle of conflicting standards in society generally. The two most prominent 'double standards' are between males and females and homosexuals and heterosexuals. For instance it's all right for your son to 'sow his wild oats' and get some sexual experience but not for your daughter. The age of consent for sexual intercourse is sixteen, for heterosexuals only; for male homosexuals to have sex together it is still twenty-one, with no legal restrictions at all on lesbians.

Traditional sexual roles have been seriously challenged with the emergence of Women's Lib but some of the possible bad effects are more aggressive, demanding and dissatisfied women, more impotent men and a possible increase in pornography which essentially seeks to degrade women.

We have already noted that adolescence is a particularly vulnerable time for hypochondriacal worries; this is especially so in the sexual sphere, with the rapid bodily changes and upsurge of powerful emotions. Puberty marks the beginning of adolescence, heralded in the girl by the start of her periods and in the boy by the voice breaking and other changes. These changes can include a large growth spurt, accompanied by apparent clumsiness and awkwardness. Facial changes such as blushing, beard growth and acne. He may worry that he hasn't as much beard growth as other boys or when, or how often to shave. Spontaneous daytime erections, sometimes occurring when in motion, such as on a bus, can also be embarrassing. The growth of the penis and whether or not to retract the foreskin, along with the appearance of smegma (bits of cheesy material round the end of the penis and under the foreskin) may also concern him.

Apart from lack of information the mere timing of puberty can bring problems as the one thing adolescents do not want is to be different from their friends. So girls worry if they haven't started their periods at the same time as others in their class (the age range is at least ten to sixteen anyway) or that their breasts are too small or too big. This latter can cause stooping, arms folded across the chest a lot, embarrassment in changing rooms and when or whether to wear a bra.

What girls expect with their periods (the 'curse' already implies it's going to be unpleasant) may well determine what actually happens. Mother's attitude and reactions are important here. If the girl is led to expect pain, headaches, sickness, fainting, no games, swimming or sports—in other words treated as an illness rather than as a natural function—she'll undoubtedly start to feel ill.

For boys there are other worries. One source of anxiety which is rarely mentioned is some soreness of the nipples and a slight swelling of the breasts (due to quite normal hormonal changes). This can worry a boy so much that he may even wonder if he's changing sex. Quite early on boys begin to worry about their virility and masculinity, when to get into long trousers and start shaving, but at the same time to be embarrassed by daytime erections and wet dreams.

Boys will also compare the shape and size of their penis with other boys' and may worry because they are not circumcised. Later on another hypochondriacal complaint may be that the penis is 'not big enough'. When asked 'not big enough for what?' the answer is usually 'not big enough to satisfy a woman'. This may so play on his mind and make him so sensitive and ashamed of his small penis that he may refuse a medical examination or to go into hospital for an operation in case nurses and others see it (another worry is that an erection might happen under similar circumstances). This may reflect a general feeling of inferiority, as penises come in all shapes and sizes and satisfying a woman depends on clitoral stimulation which has little to do with size of penis.

Masturbation (self-stimulation, playing with yourself) is still a source of guilt feelings and hypochondriacal concern in both sexes. It does not cause spots on the face, dark rings round the eyes, blindness, headaches, constant tiredness, poor school work, madness, impotence or sterility. It is, in fact, highly abnormal never to have masturbated in your life. It is a perfectly normal sexual outlet and does no harm and may well still be indulged in after marriage. Girls probably do masturbate just as much as boys and may get stimulation from activities such as horse riding. The only dangers are in using objects, as opposed to fingers, pushed into the vagina, which may be dirty or cause minor injury.

Recent views on sexual 'fulfilment', particularly in women, have also caused problems. Such are the swings of fashion that in Victorian times women were made to feel guilty if they did have an orgasm (climax) and enjoyed intercourse; now they are made to feel guilty if they don't! There is the added fear of being labelled 'frigid' or of missing something wonderful. Women then get angry and start blaming it on men for being incompetent lovers, which in turn causes further difficulties in sexual relations.

Some women don't experience orgasm until they are in their late thirties especially if they didn't start their periods until quite late. But again there is a vast range of normality, and it's perfectly possible for a woman to enjoy intercourse without reaching orgasm. Indeed to expect one every time is unrealistic. Painful intercourse may be due to some minor gynaecological trouble, but more commonly is due to spasm of the vaginal muscles and an inability to relax.

For men orgasm is usually only too easy to achieve along with ejaculation, so that a common complaint is that he 'comes' too quickly before his partner has had enough time to get properly aroused. Many men are now so uptight about their ability to satisfy a woman and feel so ashamed when they don't, that women are led to pretend to reach a climax or excuses are made to avoid intercourse altogether, sometimes on the ground of ill-health.

Most humiliating for men is to become impotent (the inability to perform sexual intercourse). There are different forms and causes of this, but once it does occur there is always increasing anxiety in anticipation of failing again next time. As anxiety itself can be a cause of impotence, a vicious circle can soon become established. Much depends on the circumstances; for instance a quick attempt at intercourse in the back of a car when half drunk, may well end in failure. It can happen to any man on occasions.

One practical advantage of masturbation (apart from release from sexual tension and fantasies) is to help overcome premature ejaculation, which is one of the most common forms of impotence, by learning to postpone orgasm. But if impotence does become chronic then nothing undermines a man's morale more and a state of hypochondriacal depression can result. However depression, and even some of the drugs used to treat it, can also be causes of a temporary loss of sexual desire and impotence.

Worries over sexual competence can be one factor in the development of an 'engagement neurosis'. In this either one of the partners is basically unsure of himself or herself, whether he really can stand on his own two feet and leave home after all. He is usually unsure of himself sexually as well. Minor hypochondriacal symptoms such as insomnia, headaches, irritability and moodiness may occur. Characteristically the wedding date is never fixed but this is blamed on having nowhere to live or financial difficulties.

Sexual adjustment after marriage may be marred by problems over contraception or happenings on the honeymoon. This latter can get off to a bad start by the woman developing 'honeymoon cystitis', which is a painful inflammation of the bladder, possibly due to minor injuries sustained during attempts at intercourse. Hypochondriacal worries can then settle on the bladder and a condition of recurrent chronic cystitis may occur with the frequent passage of hot burning urine and some degree of infection. However it's worth remembering that anxiety can also produce a constant desire to pass small quantities of urine, without there being any infection there at all.

Another symptom which may cause trouble is vaginal discharge, especially if it is smelly. This is usually not due to V.D. but to some simple infection which is readily treatable. Some very fastidious and prudish women don't even like to touch themselves 'down there' and would never dream of inserting a sanitary tampon. So that quite normal amounts of moisture may be mistaken for a discharge and poor hygiene may result in minor infection.

In a man a discharge from the penis or a spot on it, may also cause embarrassed anguish, particularly if he has a bit of a guilty conscience. Very occasionally a urinary infection can result from having anal intercourse. But a phobia of V.D. or even a delusional conviction of having it, can occur as part of an anxiety neurosis or depressive illness.

Although there is now a lot of information available about contraception, it can still be the source of much anxiety. The birth pill has proved a great blessing but there are frequent 'scares' which put some women off taking it. The possibility of getting a thrombosis or cancer of the breast, not to mention a host of other possible side-effects from making varicose veins worse to putting on weight and depression may be offputting. Many minor hypochondriacal complaints are wrongly blamed on the pill. One of the many benefits is making periods painless and regular. Even if one Pill does not suit you, there are several others available of slightly different composition which can be tried. Some apparently 'rational' explanations for not taking the Pill may hide others which are barely admitted or even recognized. Some men object because they are secretly afraid their partners would then be much more open to 'temptation' and could easily be unfaithful. Others resent the women having control over the situation or are perhaps nervous of being tricked into pregnancy by her 'forgetting' to take her Pill. Some women may insist on the man wearing a sheath as well, just to make sure or really because she doesn't like the mess of seminal fluid.

A once popular form of contraception was 'coitus interruptus' ('withdrawal') which has acquired a bad reputation for causing many neurotic symptoms. It doesn't, but on the other hand it is not a reliable method nor the best way to enjoy intercourse.

A permanent way of avoiding pregnancy is by being sterilized. In the female this can be done by having the (fallopian) tubes tied or by hysterectomy (removal of the womb). A man can have a vasectomy operation. These operations should not be undertaken lightly and even though in a few cases they can be reversed, they should be regarded as permanent. Nor should they be done to try and solve sexual problems or to save a rocky marriage. If done for the wrong reasons and without proper information and counselling, hypochondriacal symptoms can result.

A hysterectomy may be required for gynaecological reasons, often relatively minor ones, so that it doesn't mean you've got cancer. Normally the ovaries are left behind, so that symptoms of the change of life should not follow. But 'having everything taken away' or '*the* operation' is much feared by some women and can be responsible for precipitating a state of hypochondriacal depression.

The menopause, too, is often approached with very mixed feelings with so many things attributed to 'the change'. A lot depends on your personality and what you have been led to expect. Many welcome it, at least no more periods and completely natural freedom from further worries about possible pregnancy. Or you may dread it as you have been led to believe all sorts of things will happen to you like growing a moustache, the end of sexy feelings, growing fat and ugly and ceasing to be attractive to your husband.

The majority of women pass through the menopause, just as they started their periods, with no trouble at all. Nevertheless hot flushes do occur and may be embarrassing. Recent publicity over hormone replacement has led some women to expect eternal youth, but this is not possible. If your hormones have got a bit out of step you will need medical advice before starting any replacement treatment. But do not expect miracles. Hormones can certainly help hot flushes, sweats and dryness of the vagina but there is no guarantee that insomnia, fatigue, poor concentration, or loss of interest in sex will be helped without other treatment as well.

A recent survey of a group of women aged 40–55 years old found that there was no specific combination of signs and symptoms associated with the cessation of their periods, though after the menopause insomnia and hypochondriacal preoccupations were more common. Frequent symptoms were headaches, nausea, indigestion, heartburn, breathlessness and palpitations. The possibility of having cancer was the commonest preoccupation. Now that life expectancy has gone up it could be a change of life in a very general sense, for the better, and you should be looking to the future rather than thinking the best years of your life are over. You will have a new freedom to do some of the things you have always wanted to do; even though your children have grown up and left home, you may have grandchildren to look forward to.

The male menopause or 'mid-life crisis' is psychologically, rather like a second adolescence, as it is essentially concerned with taking stock of achievements and ambitions, self-esteem and career, with a realization that big changes are ahead, like retirement. There is some lowering of male sex hormone (testosterone) levels but this is very gradual and partly dependent on sexual activity, so that the best way of keeping your sex life going is to keep going! There are other bodily changes to contend with, like 'middle age spread'. Financial worries may loom large and your marriage may have got into a bit of a rut with a great temptation to have a last fling. All this may be accompanied by variable degrees of anxiety, depression and hypochondriacal concern. This is not inevitable but more common than people realize.

A fear of developing homosexual tendencies may occur at any age and in both sexes, but is most frequent in the young male. In any case actually being a homosexual is perfectly compatible with good health, both mental and physical.

Other fears may develop around ideas that you are 'kinky', a pervert or grossly abnormal. This may be because on occasions you have wanted to or have actually indulged in oral sex, anal sex or different positions in sexual intercourse. Or you may have bought some dirty magazines or indulged in all sorts of sexual daydreams and fantasies. It is very common to think about or even enjoy reading about things, such as sadistic acts, which you would never actually do in practice.

As has been mentioned more than once in this book normal human behaviour encompasses a vast range and no more so than in sexual behaviour. Sexual behaviour involving some form of commitment to another person, which both find acceptable and pleasurable, in which neither is exploited nor hurt and in which no disease is spread and no unwanted pregnancy results, is surely normal. It should not produce shame, guilt or hypochondria.

# II

# The Body Beautiful

At any one time our awareness of our bodies varies enormously and depends on age, sex, personality and mood, amongst other things. There is a constant flow of information from all parts of our bodies up to the brain. A special area of the brain integrates all these sensations and initiates actions in various muscle groups. As can be shown by stimulating various areas of the brain with an electrical current, the body is represented in an interesting way, rather like a very deformed dwarf upside down! Certain regions of the body, like the hand, thumb, face and genitals, have relatively large areas of the brain devoted to them. The nerve pathways also cross over before reaching their final destination, so that the right side of the brain controls the left side of the body and vice versa.

A resulting 'body image', that is the conscious and unconscious picture that you have of your body is built up in the brain from all the sensory information it can gather. This then acts as a system of reference for all bodily activities. For women this is subject to far greater change, for instance during pregnancy and to a lesser extent during the monthly cycle. It is not surprising that pregnant women become more body conscious and prone to develop hypochondriacal worries, not only about themselves but also about the baby growing inside them. In premenstrual tension, usually at its worst during the week before the period is due, a certain amount of bodily swelling occurs, when you feel bloated with tender breasts and a tight wedding ring. This may be accompanied by a variable degree of tension, irritability and depression.

We have already noted a certain relationship between body build and personality. 'Body language' is a very primitive mode of expression, a form of non-verbal communication through bodily movements; speaking with your muscles rather than your mouth. So we can get very complicated relationships between our feelings and our bodies, which are very relevant to a better understanding of hypochondriacal symptoms.

We may also affect our bodies by what we do to them, this in turn being very much under the influence of current fads and fashions and commercial pressures. Vanity is important here, especially in women, although it's worth noting that the technical name for morbid self-love is narcissism, derived from the Greek myth of Narcissus who was *male* and fell in love with his own reflection! As already mentioned this tendency is traditionally associated with an hysterical personality. This may also influence a woman's decision about breast feeding or indeed pregnancy itself if she thinks it might ruin her figure (it could even improve it).

Women are very much 'slaves of fashion' (so often designed by men!) and no more so than adolescent girls. They will cripple themselves with unsuitable shoes, ruin their hair and faces, and generally wear anything even if it's uncomfortable and unhealthy, so long as it's in fashion, which means all the others are doing the same.

Ideas of beauty also change and are very much mixed up with sex appeal. It is again the female who sets the standard; other women admire 'beautiful' women, would like to be like them, and know that they are at the same time attractive to the opposite sex. Male parades of health and strength appeal more to male homosexuals than to women.

The current fashion is for the slim, 'boyish' look, so that diet and fears of getting fat are common preoccupations. The most serious abnormality here, which seems to be getting more frequent, is the condition of 'compulsive slimming' called, medically, anorexia nervosa.

This is a bad name as anorexia, which means loss of appetite, is not found; what occurs is a selective loss of appetite for fattening foods only, at least in the early stages. There is a phobia of getting fat. There are probably many minor cases which get better themselves. A young girl gets teased at school for being fat, perhaps she has put on a bit of 'puppy fat'. She gets miserable ('fed-up') about this and goes on a diet. It seems that she can't stop and it gets out of hand, but after some months she begins to eat more normally again.

It is middle-class girls, aged sixteen onwards who are mostly affected by anorexia nervosa (it does occur in boys but it is very rare) and it could well be related to our affluent and over-nourished society. This in turn promotes rapid physical maturity, especially amongst girls, who then associate fatness with other adolescent problems. There is now an almost universal tendency amongst female adolescents to diet in some way; this is not found in boys. There are, as well, particular problems facing today's adolescents, which do not help their development.

In essence what these girls really fear, deep down, is growing up and adult sexuality. By becoming so thin they in effect retard their growth, lose their attractiveness and revert to pre-puberty as their periods stop. By getting so emaciated they eventually suppress their own appetites, both sexual and for food. There is (to others) a frightening oblivion to what they are doing to themselves and what they really look like. This is a real disorder of the 'body image', as they can look like walking skeletons yet express satisfaction with their bodies.

Undoubtedly the brain and the hormones are involved, as shown by the periods stopping and sometimes by the growth of a fine downy hair on the body. How else she reacts depends, once again, on personality type, whether this is predominantly obsessional, hysterical or anxious and immature. She may also get quite depressed but most get very 'deceitful' and will do anything to avoid gaining weight. For example she will hide her food, make herself vomit, secretly take laxatives or maintain a high degree of physical activity. She will try and make sure her true weight is kept a secret and will wear trousers and long sleeves to hide her stick-like limbs. She will frequently deny any problems. In extreme cases it can be seen as a slow suicide, for it is possible to starve yourself to death. These more severe cases require expert treatment in hospital.

The opposite problem of obesity is again much more commonly complained of by women than men. Women may overeat for a variety of reasons; boredom, frustration, anxiety and depression being some of them. It is found more often in poorer people because fattening foods (mostly carbohydrates) are usually cheaper and they may not be so well informed about dietetics.

It is easy to get trapped in a vicious circle of overeating and depression. Once overweight you become prone to develop other complications such as shortness of breath, backache, arthritis and other aches and pains. Certain people do seem to have marked 'oral dependency' needs, which means, rather like a frustrated baby, they always have to be stuffing something in their mouths as a dummy or comforter, be it food, sweets, drink, pills or cigarettes. Some women pick at food all day but can still honestly say they don't eat big meals. There are now a number of self-help groups, like Weight Watchers, which try and help people to stick to a sensible diet.

Apart from obesity you may think there are other things wrong with your body, like being too tall, too short or having feet that are too big. There is a whole group of hypochondriacal conditions which go under the name of an 'ugliness complex'. With women it can be their breasts, either too small or too large and pendulous. With either sex the ears, chin or nose may be complained of. In very sensitive and self-conscious individuals and adolescents, even though to others there's not much wrong that they can see, to the person concerned it seems to ruin their whole life.

This is one of the difficulties as it is so much easier to blame your big nose for all your troubles rather than 'face up' to the fact that it's really because you're shy, awkward, insecure, lonely and lacking in personal graces. In other words, 'it's nothing to do with me as a person only my blessed nose', and who really likes to admit their own personal inadequacies. Following this way of thinking the easy way out (and often the wrong one) would seem to be to get a new nose by plastic surgery. But in such cases it's no use expecting that by some magic operation you will automatically become a different person overnight and have a happier life.

In other cases, when there is apparently nothing really wrong that can be seen by others, the person may be deluded, seriously depressed or believe that people laugh at him behind his back, point him out in the street and make unkind remarks. This is why plastic surgeons have to be very careful who they operate on. If it is the wrong person, more harm than good can result. But in the right cases there is no doubt that it can be a tremendous boost to morale to look less conspicuous or more attractive. However pure 'cosmetic' surgery, like a face-lift, is only available under the National Health Service if it is necessary in the interests of your health.

Other parts of your body, especially those bits obvious to all like skin and hair can also feature in the 'ugliness complex'. The face is an important area where even a minor blemish can cause great unhappiness. Spots generally and acne in particular worry most adolescents at some time or other. There is always the temptation to pick and squeeze, and so often they seem to get worse just before an important event, like going to a disco. There can be a flare-up during the time just before a period is due and certainly when tense and anxious. Occasionally scars can be left which require special treatment.

So often you are told that you'll grow out of it, which is not always true nor does it help much then and there and is no substitute for sympathetic advice on the care of your skin. Although acne is associated with the sex hormones (particularly androgens or male ones, which both sexes have quite normally) sexual activity or lack of it has no direct effect.

But there is some connection between the type of skin you have and your personality. Some have a more oily or greasy skin, which provides a background for a number of skin troubles which, although not serious or catching, can cause hypochondriacal worries. Acne, scurf (dandruff) and a tendency to fungus infections between the toes (athlete's foot) and the groin are some of them. Clever advertising plays on social embarrassment and implies that if you use a particular brand of shampoo, you will straight away become the life and soul of the party and meet Prince Charming on your first evening out.

Things like birth marks, warts, varicose veins and other skin blemishes can either be removed, disguised with cover-up cosmetics, or otherwise treated. Other infections such as 'cold sores' on the lips and mouth ulcers do tend to recur, as boils sometimes do. Many of these very common but non-serious conditions can be very depressing. And it seems, rather like colds and 'flu, we really don't know very much about what causes them.

A related problem is that of blushing, which to some

very sensitive people makes social life a misery. Certain types of skin where the blood vessels are near the surface and easily seen, as well as an over-reactive nervous system, can combine to produce easy flushing. Teasing only increases the problem. It is an awful mixture of wanting to be noticed but at the same time not wanting to stand out from the crowd. The picture of the sweet innocent girl, who charmingly averts her gaze and blushes, is all very romantic but in actual fact if you were entirely innocent (and terribly immature!) you wouldn't have any cause to blush. Fears of blushing can be overcome although in itself it's a quite normal reaction.

There is a much more extended area of the skin, down the neck and upper chest, which is a potential 'flush' area. This may come out in itchy blotches or a general flush when you get 'hot and bothered' and occasionally as part of an allergic reaction. This area is the one most affected in menopausal hot flushes. Some other skin diseases may give the appearance of a permanent blush or red nose, which others (wrongly) may attribute to drinking or sexual guilt, only causing you further embarrassment.

Skin diseases in general, especially on exposed areas of the body, can cause a 'leper complex', even when the condition is perfectly harmless. A good example is psoriasis, which occurs on the knees and elbows, causing flaking skin and pink, raw-looking areas. On the other hand some people with deep-seated conflicts actually produce skin rashes by excessive scratching or otherwise cutting or burning themselves, often even denying they've done it themselves. Others still may feel strange sensations in their skin, like fine sand being blown on to it or like crawling insects or worms. Drugs such as cocaine can be responsible.

Excessive sweating, unsuitable clothing, poor hygiene and anxiety may all contribute to itching which may be confined to specific areas, like round the anus and genitals and be very distressing and embarrassing. This is what one recent advertisement very coyly referred to as 'personal membrane itching'. Other relevant factors may be infection, allergy, an irritating discharge or piles. Generalized itching is sometimes part of a depressive illness.

Hair has an obvious sexual significance and how it's displayed, not displayed or removed is very much subject to fashion. Baldness is sometimes feared and anxious hypochondriacal people will begin to notice hair coming out in 'fistfuls' or in their combs. A certain amount comes away anyway but once you start to worry about it you begin to take more notice. Others, including children, may pull out their hair or constantly rub bald patches, as a nervous habit. The typical male pattern of baldness, with receding hair line is normal and depends on male sex hormones (as is often pointed out, eunuchs never go bald, if that's any comfort to you!) so in that sense it shows you're normal. It cannot be 'cured' or altered. At what age and at what speed it develops as well as in what particular way is probably hereditary.

A general thinning out of the hair is normal in both sexes with increasing age. Total baldness (eyebrows, pubic hair, the lot) can occur but is extremely rare in otherwise healthy individuals. Going 'grey' is another cause for concern to some; it signifies old age and by implication death. To others it is distinguished looking and welcome. Stories of turning white overnight from some sudden shock or worry are a myth.

General hairiness in women can cause problems, especially if the hair is very dark and shows up easily, although the amount of body hair varies enormously. To some this is very sexy, to others it's too masculine and ugly, and much, as always, depends on what's fashionable. A slight 'moustache' or hair on the face, round the base of the nipples or up the middle of the tummy, occur very frequently in women. Very rarely is extreme hairiness a sign of hormonal imbalance or illness. It's mostly a matter of personal choice and there are now many ways of getting rid of unwanted hair if this is desired.

Finally trouble over the eyes and teeth can mar the body beautiful. Correction of a bad squint or 'lazy eye' can help self-confidence and although glasses are often quickly assimilated into the 'body image' there may be trouble, particularly in girls. This might increase a girl's fear that she is not attractive enough, or indeed be made a further excuse for not mixing, rather than admit to excessive shyness. A constant preoccupation or apparent sensitivity to bright light with the need to wear tinted glasses (? rose coloured!) may well hide deeper neurotic anxieties.

Contact lenses may be sought to try to avoid some of these difficulties, even having tinted ones to alter the colour of your eyes. But just as some people are always fussing over and fidgeting with their glasses, they may do just the same with contact lenses. They need looking after, can take a lot of getting used to, can be costly and may produce new worries, for instance that will they fall into the soup!

Buck teeth or other obvious abnormalities should be corrected early in life, even though there might be a fear of dentists or a dislike of wearing a brace. Correctly fitting false teeth with advice over their care could prevent a lot of social embarrassment and unnecessary worry.

## 12

## Bother the Doctors?

Should you go and see your doctor or not? As already noted much depends on your personality but also how ill you feel, how long you have been ill, what you think may be wrong and how disabled you are.

Hypochondriacs do like to talk about their health, grumble about it and perhaps even bore others with it. When you get the usual greeting, 'how are you?' do you take this up and really describe how you are? There are many other possible sources of advice, apart from doctors: friends, relatives, your wife or husband are obvious ones. But those near to you may have heard it all before so may not be so ready to lend a sympathetic ear or to give you the re-assurance you need.

There is, too, the problem of 'crying wolf'. You could have made rather a fuss over relatively trivial complaints in the past, but now when you feel it's much more serious nobody takes any notice. Your barmaid or hairdresser may get quite used to hearing about other people's worries during the course of their work. But perhaps the person most consulted is a chemist. He's fine for minor things like wanting something for a sore throat, bunion or scurf, but you cannot expect him to be able to diagnose all your aches and pains.

Magazines and books are further sources of help. Your local library no doubt stocks some popular medical books which you can consult but be careful of searching through too many medical dictionaries and encyclopaedias because you will soon convince yourself that you've got everything under the sun. Magazines which run a problem page or regular health articles frequently get letters from readers with queries about their health. These may be of a very personal nature or things which you are particularly embarrassed or shy about. Magazines run all the way from the general ones for women, which nearly always have something about health and beauty to specialized ones for sexual problems only.

Television and radio regularly produce educational and documentary programmes about health matters but usually do not answer specific questions, except occasionally in phone-in programmes. Although there is a stringent code of practice for advertising, many of the T.V. commercials do tend to play on the least desirable aspects of your character and still use sex appeal and other possible 'rewards' to persuade you to buy their particular products.

Your priest or minister is another source of help. Many are now taught counselling techniques as part of their training. There may also be social activities connected with the Church, which can be a further source of support, especially if you are lonely.

There are other groups available, with trained personnel, whom you can consult about specific problems, such as the Marriage Guidance Council and social workers from your local authority Social Services Department. If you are feeling desperate or suicidal the Samaritans run a twenty-four-hour telephone answering service in most large towns.

A modern trend has been the formation of self-help groups, often started by a single person or small group of people either themselves suffering from the condition or having near relatives who do. An additional impetus to forming the group may have been dissatisfaction with orthodox medical treatment facilities. There are a very large number of such groups available but the difficulty is getting to know about them. It's possible that your local Citizens Advice Bureau may have the addresses of some local ones. Perhaps it's time for hypochondriacs to form their own?

Well-meaning friends may tell you, or indeed you may tell yourself, to pull yourself together. This can be exactly the opposite from what you should really be doing, that is letting yourself go more, not taking life and yourself quite so seriously and learning to relax. One way of doing this is to join a Yoga class.

Changing your habits, way of life or environment may all be helpful. If you've never had a proper holiday and feel you're indispensable, it's time to change. You will do yourself and others with whom you work much more good by taking a well-earned break and going back refreshed. Have a second honeymoon, do something you've never done before, get out of yourself and stop thinking about yourself so much.

If you must keep thinking about yourself be more positive about it—the old-fashioned 'auto-suggestion' had much to commend it—say to yourself, 'every day and in every way I'm getting better and better'. Everybody knows about physical fitness but your mind may also need proper exercising and discipline. You can learn some mental discipline to control your morbid thoughts. Say 'stop' to yourself, at first out loud and bang something down like a rolled-up newspaper on the table, to emphasize the point. Then learn to say it quietly to yourself, then just think it. Wear an elastic band round your wrist and as soon as you begin to think morbid thoughts, give the band a ping, just enough to sting yourself to stop.

Take up a hobby or go to evening classes. Another good way of helping yourself is to help others, by voluntary work, assisting with school dinners, the W.V.S. or some local charity.

When it comes to treating yourself with pills and medicines, do be careful, as apart from wasting your money, you can do yourself a lot of harm. Many patent medicines, 'tonics', vitamin preparations and such like, if they work at all, do so mainly by what is called a 'placebo' effect. Placebo means 'I shall please' and refers to the non-specific effects of a drug or the power of a totally inert substance to produce effects. In other words if you have faith in it and believe it's going to help you, it probably will at least to a certain extent, even though it's only coloured chalk. High price, 'testimonials' to its power, impressive packaging, colour, shape and nasty taste, all help to make you think it's going to do you good. Highly suggestible people can even get undesirable 'side-effects', like feeling sleepy or a headache, from a placebo.

Do not take aspirins or other pain killers, sleeping pills or slimming pills, on a regular basis without consulting a doctor. You may get hooked on them and there can be dangerous long-term side-effects. Totally avoid 'pep-pills' or anything else you may be offered 'under the counter' or by strangers in bars or cafés. There is no such thing as a safe, medically approved aphrodisiac (to make you feel sexy), which really works. Nor should you need to take laxatives on a regular basis or need a regular 'clean out' at certain times.

Do not waste your money, either, on 'tonic' wines, herbal preparations or special 'energy giving' drinks or foods. Yoghurt will not prolong life, but may well be a pleasant way of getting milk without too much fat. Other 'health foods' are really a matter of personal taste. Health 'farms', hotels, spas and other 'medicinal' holidays should also be treated with caution. If you want a safe, reliable and properly balanced slimming diet ask your doctor or hospital dietitian.

If you suffer from indigestion, temporary relief may be produced by taking antacids and other similar medicines freely available at your chemist. But if symptoms persist, see your doctor, as it is much more sensible to treat causes rather than symptoms. Also doctors can prescribe cheaper, safer and more proven remedies than you can buy over the counter. The same argument applies to a persistent cough; do not keep on trying different cough cures.

If you are feeling tired and generally run down, don't go dosing yourself up with extra vitamins and iron pills. If you are really anaemic, the only way to find out is to have a simple blood test, and in any case, it is very important to find out what sort of anaemia it is.

There is a whole industry devoted to beauty and slimming aids, and a lot of money made out of dubious claims, sometimes so cleverly or vaguely worded that it is hard to show they are contravening any law. It is, for instance, extremely difficult, if not impossible, to slim down only certain parts of your body, like your hips or your bottom, and there is no safe and proven medicine which will dissolve fat.

You may feel bitter that nobody cares and even the doctors have given you up as a bad job. But beware of being exploited by others who are only in business to make money and do not necessarily have your welfare at heart. Some can be quite unscrupulous, have no professional training of any sort or ethical standards. Hypochondriacs are especially vulnerable to being exploited by all manner of 'fringe' healers.

There are a whole host of them, faith healers, nature healers, unregistered massage parlours and manipulators, quasi-religious groups, acupuncturists, chiropractors and osteopaths, to name but a few. If you do decide to see an osteopath, say for chronic neck or back pain, make sure he's a registered one as this means he has at least had four years' training. You can find out from the General Osteopathic Register in London.

There are others who advertise in the small ads of

various magazines as 'psychologists', hypnotists, psycho-
therapists and the like, who will claim to cure your bad
nerves, blushing, inferiority complex and hypochondria.
Again be very careful both financially and otherwise about
what you may be letting yourself in for. There is no guarantee that any of these have had any proper training, in spite
of impressive looking letters after their names.

So how about seeing your family doctor after all? You've
seen him before and you don't want to bother him again?
He's not very understanding or sympathetic? Always gives
you some more pills? He'll only send you to out-patients?
And so on. How many more excuses can you think of?

How much you benefit from and trust your doctor obviously depends, up to a point, on what sort of doctor he is
and even more importantly on what sort of person he is.
But it also depends on your attitudes and expectations as
well. Some people are quite unrealistic, they still see the
doctor as a kind of modern miracle man, who can rescue
them and rid them of all their pains and troubles. When he
doesn't live up to these expectations you get angry and
despondent.

Of course there can be a clash of personalities or your
doctor seems to be better at treating more straightforward
medical and surgical things and is not so good on nervous
disorders. He may seem remote and inaccessible or just the
opposite, very much a family friend so that you might even
hesitate in confiding in him about a very personal matter.
There are many other possibilities, but bear in mind you
can always change your doctor and he in turn, can take you
off his list.

Then there is the problem of communication. How can
you get across to him, in a short time, in the middle of a
busy surgery, just what is worrying you? Will he understand and get the message? A lot of people think the average
family doctor is more interested in their bodies than their

personal worries and finer feelings and so you may 'present' him with your headache or other physical complaint to gain his interest and attention. What you really want to tell him is that you feel frightened and depressed in case you've got cancer, or that you're feeling sexually frustrated because your husband is impotent, but hope that somehow he will guess what's really worrying you. In other words you present him with some physical complaint in order to strike up a dialogue, during the course of which you hope other matters will come to light. If this doesn't happen you go away feeling dissatisfied.

On the other hand you must be fair to your doctor. He can't read your thoughts, he's not possessed of any magical intuition, and even after many years' experience he may not immediately cotton on to what is really troubling you. It's far better to come out with it straight away. He will not laugh at you, criticize you, think you're making a lot of fuss about nothing or wasting his time.

Even if you know your doctor very well, and for that matter his receptionist, nurse and everybody else concerned with his practice, you need not worry about confidentiality. This can sometimes be used as an excuse for not facing up to the real problem. All members of the health team are very concerned about professional secrecy; all case files are carefully guarded and no doctor will pass on confidential information about you to anyone else (except other doctors or specialists so they can help you) without your permission. You needn't worry about them finding out at work either, as all official certificates are deliberately worded rather vaguely. If you are aged sixteen and over, then you are treated like an adult and can make up your own mind about having any treatment and your parents will not be informed without your consent.

Looked at from the doctor's point of view there are several problems. One of these is time. The average length of a consultation in general practice is about six minutes, although many doctors will realize that a special, longer appointment, may well be better in the long run and preferable to many short ones. He must also be careful not to make you worse, in the sense of suggesting other symptoms to you, either by asking you too many leading questions, doing too many tests and investigations or in the way he examines you. For example he may, after taking your blood pressure, start asking you about headaches and may even seem a bit cross when you deny having any. But if you are that sort of person, you may then start getting headaches, even when, at least with mild degrees of high blood pressure, it's quite unusual.

The doctor has to strike a very difficult balance between, on the one hand, your going away disgruntled thinking he has not taken you seriously or you haven't been examined properly and, on the other, overdoing it or giving you the impression that he's not sure himself and that there must be something seriously wrong. Either he or you may want a second opinion. Further investigations at the hospital, a visit to the out-patient department to see a specialist, may of course be necessary.

Again communication is very important. The doctor may have had a very different education and background from you and find it difficult to explain things to you in a way you can understand; this even more so when either of you come from another country.

When your own doctor says to you there's nothing wrong with you, what he really means is there's nothing *seriously* wrong with you. If there was nothing at all wrong with you, you wouldn't be there in the first place and that ache in your chest, dry mouth and pounding heart must be due to something. Similarly if he says to you, it's only your nerves, don't misunderstand him. We have already seen that the symptoms just mentioned could be due to anxiety and that is what he is telling you. What he does *not* mean is that he thinks you're imagining it, putting it on, making a fuss about nothing or you're going round the bend.

It's a popular complaint that 'they never tell you anything' meaning doctors in general and hospital doctors in particular. Sometimes, of course, this is true but so often it's because you're anxious and when you are very anxious (and most people are a bit anxious anyway over seeing a doctor) it can affect your attention and concentration. In other words you often are told things but because you're in a bit of a state, you don't take it in.

Another thing which you may well expect (and the doctor expects you to expect, another vicious circle!) is treatment in the form of a bottle of medicine or pills. In fact you may feel cheated if not given something after your visit. Doctors know this and because they themselves are frequently under pressure, both from the time point of view and also from the pharmaceutical industry, too many prescriptions are given. It's a lot easier, on both sides, to have sleeping pills, rather than go into the possible reasons why you've got insomnia. It maybe is only a passing phase that will right itself and you stop taking the pills when the bottle is empty and no harm is done.

But if the insomnia persists and you begin to live off repeat prescriptions without ever having tried to tackle the root causes, this is bad medicine. Although eventually both you and your doctor, after trying to solve any underlying worries may reach some sort of understanding, without ever putting it into words, that after all a bottle of pills is the best form of communication between you and the best way of helping you.

On the other hand all pills and medicines, if they really work have 'side-effects', that is unwanted effects like making you feel a bit sleepy in the daytime. A few people are especially sensitive or allergic to certain drugs. With all the powerful drugs available today you can sometimes get into a mess as some drug side-effects may be very similar to the symptoms you are trying to treat.

There is also the possibility of getting hooked on them. With many drugs, even if your body does not get hooked your mind can, so the pills become a kind of crutch or prop which you come to rely on and find you can't face life without. We have already discussed placebos and many drugs, although they will have passed stringent safety tests, may not work in the way they are claimed to. Much again depends on the doctor's personality and enthusiasm as well as your own. However no doctor will knowingly play tricks on you and deliberately prescribe a placebo, as after all the main basis for any treatment is for you to have a relationship of mutual trust.

Many doctors now work in a team with a Health Visitor or Community Nurse, who can visit you at home. Don't think you are being 'fobbed off' with second best, as these other workers have been specially trained and can, when and if necessary always call in the doctor again or consult him on your behalf. In fact a sympathetic Health Visitor or similar person attached to a general practice, can do much to help you cope with such everyday problems as may be getting you down.

One of the things your doctor may do is to refer you to a psychiatrist. Don't immediately get into a panic or on your high horse, and start thinking 'am I that bad?' 'so he thinks I'm mad does he?' or 'it's not all in the mind'. There is nothing to fear and just because a psychiatrist deals with 'mental' cases it doesn't necessarily mean you're one or about to have a nervous breakdown. Much of the stigma attached to the old-fashioned lunatic asylum or mental hospital has now gone and in any case many psychiatrists can be consulted in general hospitals or out-patient clinics.

A psychiatrist is medically qualified and has undergone

several years of postgraduate training. You can tell a fully qualified one by the letters after his name which will be either D.P.M. (Diploma of Psychological Medicine) or M.R.C.Psych. (Member of the Royal College of Psychiatrists). A person who is not medically qualified may not call himself a psychiatrist.

The popular (fictional) idea of one with his horn-rimmed glasses, piercing eyes, thick mid-European accent, suave and eccentric manner, who can read your thoughts at a glance, is not met with in real life. Neither does he use a couch for the initial consultation, this is only used by some psychoanalysts (who may or may not be medically qualified) for treatment. A psychologist or clinical psychologist, the one you are most likely to meet, works with the psychiatrist and helps with both diagnosis and treatment. He has a university degree and has also undergone special postgraduate training but is not medically qualified, although he may have a Ph.D (Doctor of Philosophy) or equivalent degree, which does entitle him to be called doctor.

There are many jokes about psychiatrists (head shrinker, trick cyclist etc.) which often imply they're a bit crazy themselves, because this is one way of dealing with somebody we are not quite sure about and even a little bit afraid of. The modern psychiatrist, even though he's no different from any other medical specialist is still seen as part magician, priest, father figure and confessor, who knows how to tame dark and little understood forces. However, many of our expectations are not met for the simple reason that they never can be. We can easily project onto the psychiatrist a lot of our own unrecognized faults and fears and when the magic wand or equivalent is not forthcoming, we tend to feel frustrated and resentful.

What happens at a psychiatric consultation? Although there are obviously some differences in different parts of the country, the basic pattern is much the same everywhere. You will be asked to attend one of the psychiatrist's out-patient clinics where you will sit in an ordinary chair, face to face, and most of the time will be spent in him asking you for further details about your present complaints and your previous history. This is just like seeing a specialist physician, except it takes longer, as more details are required, including a potted biography of yourself.

Indeed psychiatrists and family doctors are about the only doctors left now who are interested in you as a person, all of you, mind and body and not just a little bit of you like your kidneys or heart. This means that some of the questions cover sensitive and personal areas, such as your sexual development. Because you are asked a lot of personal details psychiatrists are even more aware of the importance of confidentiality. They must write down some of your history but the notes are very carefully guarded, and details only made available, if relevant, to others concerned with your treatment. And no personal details will be given to any other person, including whoever may come with you, without your permission.

It is helpful to the psychiatrist if somebody who knows you well comes along with you to your first appointment. This is to help build up a picture of what sort of person you are normally and how you seem to have changed. Even with the best will in the world it's terribly difficult to be objective about yourself and especially so if you are emotionally upset. For instance if you are depressed you may give a very gloomy picture of yourself, so you can see that a friend's or relative's account could be helpful in giving a more balanced view.

As we have seen, many of your problems, although mainly presenting as physical complaints often have complicated causes in a number of different areas such as physical, emotional and social. Just as causes are multiple so is treatment and this involves others using their special skills and training to help you. So most psychiatrists also work in a team, other members of which, apart from junior doctors, will be nurses, social worker, psychologist and occupational therapist. The psychiatrist heads the team and as he and his junior assistants are all doctors, any physical problems or investigations can also be undertaken or if more complicated other specialists will be called in to help. A physical examination, if not already done by your family doctor before referral, may also be part of the initial psychiatric consultation.

The types of treatment available will now be briefly summarized. First of all assessment and advice, when only one visit may be necessary. Just being able to tell someone, often for the first time, about all your problems and your life may in itself make you feel a lot better. Further treatment may be necessary but in many cases can be supervised by your own family doctor with appropriate advice from the psychiatrist.

More specialized psychiatric treatment is available on an out-patient basis or in some parts of the country at a Day Hospital. As the name suggests you attend just for the day and do not sleep there and do not attend as a rule at weekends either.

For various reasons (and not necessarily because you are such a bad case) you may be offered in-patient treatment. Some forms of treatment and investigation can only be given as an in-patient. And remember that the original and nicest meaning of the word 'asylum' was a sanctuary or place of refuge, so that admission may be indicated to give you a break, to get away from it all for a while, to have a rest and give yourself the best possible chance of sorting yourself out.

Lastly further treatment in the community may be best for you, with either a community nurse, social worker or some other team member (in liaison with your family doctor), visiting you on a regular basis, at home.

This is a brief account of where treatment can be carried out. I would like to finish with an equally brief account of what kinds of treatment are available. First there is treatment with drugs such as tranquillizers, sedatives and anti-depressants, either singly or in combination. It is very important to take the drugs exactly as prescribed. Many patients do not and then get even more upset because they're no better.

You may be 'anti-pills', frightened of becoming dependent on them or seeing them as only first aid. You should discuss your fears and reservations at the time they are prescribed. They are often necessary for a limited period only, to help you over a bad patch, to enable you to think about yourself and your problems in a more constructive way or more specifically to treat a depressive illness or anxiety state.

Sometimes there are special precautions necessary, like avoiding certain foods, which will either be explained to you at the time or you will be given written instructions. Occasionally a busy doctor may forget to give you a very simple but important bit of information about taking your pills. Here are just two examples.

With many of these drugs it can be dangerous to mix them with alcohol and then drive a car, as you might get very sluggish and be unable to react quickly enough in an emergency. And when you are prescribed anti-depressants do remember that they are not pep-pills and do not act immediately; they have to be taken for at least two weeks before you begin to feel the benefit. In other words it's no use throwing them down the loo in a couple of days in a further fit of depression because you feel no better; give them a fair chance.

In spite of or perhaps because of, attempts at educating

the general public, people still very much fear E.C.T. (electroconvulsive therapy). The name is unfortunate but there is nothing frightening or experimental about it; it has been in use for nearly forty years. It is not painful, as you are given an anaesthetic and it is very safe. Like any other type of treatment it can be abused but when properly used it is a valuable and sometimes even a life-saving treatment or rather course of treatment as usually about six to eight treatments are necessary. It is most effective in the more severe forms of depression. But it won't be sprung on you and your written consent (as for any anaesthetic or operation) will be obtained first. In some centres it is given on an out-patient basis.

A most important form of treatment is psychotherapy, popularly known as the 'talking treatment'. This involves a trained person deliberately establishing a professional relationship with you, with the object of removing or modifying existing symptoms and promoting positive personality growth. There are several different types.

One type of psychotherapy is principally aimed at support and relieving distress. It builds on your own resources and helps you to function more efficiently and includes counselling, explanation, reassurance and advice about day to day problems. As with all types of psychotherapy a lot depends on the therapist's personality and how you get on with each other.

Another type of psychotherapy aims to dig a little deeper, to go back into your past life in order to help you understand yourself better, why you have developed these particular symptoms and to learn new ways of coping with stress in the future. This involves a certain amount of self-analysis but need not go as far as a radical psychoanalysis, which is a very long-term process (years), time consuming and expensive, as it is not generally available on the National Health Service.

The briefer sorts of psychotherapy, often using techniques derived from psychoanalysis, are the stock in trade of most psychiatrists and can either be individual or in groups. Psychotherapy can also be combined with other treatments, for instance a course of tranquillizers or antidepressant drugs. Treatment sessions would be for about an hour, once weekly or less frequently, on an out-patient basis and go on for several weeks or months.

Another form of treatment is called behaviour therapy, not a very good name as most forms of treatment aim to modify behaviour. This approach has been mainly developed by psychologists on the basis that many neurotic and other symptoms have been learnt, like bad habits, so that you can apply some of the rules of learning to 'unlearn' them. There are various techniques available for doing this principally aimed at combating the underlying tension and anxiety by special relaxation exercises. Also you can learn to cope with specific phobias and how to overcome those obsessional worries about health and illness and other morbid thoughts. A further modification is to negotiate a contract with you, with agreed specific goals to be achieved, which are then rewarded when you achieve them.

Hypnosis has a very limited part to play in treatment, although a few doctors are enthusiastic about it. At any rate in the sense of being put to sleep and having all your troubles, pains and symptoms 'magicked' away, it just does not work. All treatments require your active co-operation and the basic will to help yourself get better.

# Appendix

# Appendix

## SOME USEFUL NAMES AND ADDRESSES

This is a selection of the many groups and organizations that you could find helpful. Some provide useful publications or act as information centres whilst others offer practical advice, understanding, friendship or group support.

Many are registered charities and are run on a voluntary basis, often on a very limited budget. Others do charge fees either for consultations, membership or for their publications. But in any case, if you decide to write to any of them, do remember to enclose a stamped addressed envelope for a reply. Similarly, if you send for any books, allow some extra for postage and packing. As prices keep altering I have not attempted to quote the actual cost of any individual publication. Fees may well have altered too.

Even though all the details were correct at the time of writing, by the time you come to read this all sorts of changes may have taken place. For instance, some organizations may have moved or had to give up altogether through lack of funds, so I cannot offer any guarantee about this or of the service offered.

In all cases I have given the address of the headquarters of the particular organization but in many instances there will be local branches or groups. You can often check on this by consulting your local telephone directory, Citizens' Advice Bureau or Social Services Department. Just because an organization is not mentioned in my list does not necessarily imply that I do not approve of it. But I have already warned you in the book about falling into the hands of unscrupulous people. One final word of warning about cosmetic surgery; the only way to make sure that a plastic surgeon is competent and properly qualified is to go through your own doctor.

AGE CONCERN ENGLAND
Bernard Sunley House, 60 Pitcairn Road, Mitcham,
Surrey CR4 3LL
Tel: 01–640 5431

Information centre on all aspects of the welfare of old people. Local groups provide voluntary services.

ALCOHOLICS ANONYMOUS
PO Box 514, 11 Redcliffe Gardens, London, SW10
Tel: 01–352 9779

Local branches. For help over drinking problems.

ANOREXICS ANONYMOUS
24 Westmoreland Road, London, SW13

Local groups. A mutual support society for anorexics and their families.

BRENT CONSULTATION CENTRE
Johnston House, 51 Winchester Avenue, London NW6 7TT
Tel: 01–328 0918

A walk-in service for young people (age 16–23) to discuss their problems. Free and confidential advice but ongoing psychological treatment only for those who live, work or attend school in the Borough of Brent.

CONSUMERS' ASSOCIATION
14 Buckingham Street, London WC2N 6DS
Tel: 01–839 1222

Publish a range of books, available through bookshops, on such topics as Avoiding Back Trouble, Health for Old Age and Slimming Guide. Monthly magazine *Which?* available to subscribers only carries occasional critical articles on health matters. Do not deal with individual enquiries.

CRUSE CLUB
126 Sheen Road, Richmond, Surrey
Tel: 01–940 4818/9047

Local groups. Counselling service for widows, widowers and their children.

DEPRESSIVES ASSOCIATED
National Co-ordinator, Mrs Janet Stevenson, 19 Merley Ways, Wimborne Minster, Dorset BH21 1QN
Tel: (0202) 883957

Local groups. For support and help from others who have suffered a period of depression. A s.a.e. should be sent with enquiries.

FAMILY DOCTOR PUBLICATIONS
B.M.A. House, Tavistock Square, London NW1H 9JP
Tel: 01–387 9721

Publish a whole range of popular but authoritative booklets on pregnancy and childbirth, child-care management, sex education, food and diets, general health and preventive medicine, medical conditions and psychological medicine. Available at some chemists and bookshops or direct from the publishers.

FAMILY PLANNING ASSOCIATION
Margaret Pyke House, 27–35 Mortimer Street,
London W1N 7RJ
Tel: 01–636 7866

Information bureau. Medical advice and assistance for involuntary sterility, sexual and marital difficulties.

FORUM CLINIC
The Forum Personal Adviser, 2 Bramber Road,
London W14 9PB
Tel: 01–385 6181

Help, information, advice, counselling service and therapy for sexual and marital problems. Private and confidential. Consultation fee, payable in advance, £8.50. Wednesday evening clinics. Write for appointment.

HEALTH EDUCATION COUNCIL
78 New Oxford Street, London WC1A 1AH
Tel: 01–637 1881

Publish a series of free leaflets on a whole range of health matters and maintain an Information Section. Also publish a booklet on *Treating Yourself*.

LONDON YOUTH ADVISORY SERVICE
Camden Branch,
26 Prince of Wales Road, London NW5
Tel: 01–267 4792

A confidential advice and counselling service for young people (age 13–25). A small fee may be charged.

MIND (NATIONAL ASSOCIATION FOR MENTAL HEALTH)
22 Harley Street, London W1N 2ED
Tel: 01–637 0741

Social work department offers free advice on most nervous and psychiatric problems. Many useful publications on mental health from Mind/NAMH Bookshop, Mind Yorkshire Office, 157 Woodhouse Lane, Leeds LS2 3EF
Tel: (0532) 453926

THE NATIONAL MARRIAGE GUIDANCE COUNCIL
Herbert Gray College,
Little Church Street, Rugby, Warwicks CV21 3AP
Tel: Rugby 73241

Counselling service for relationship problems, especially marital, and psychosexual difficulties. Appointments through local offices. No fee but a contribution towards expenses is welcomed. Many useful publications.

NATIONAL SCHIZOPHRENIA FELLOWSHIP
78–79 Victoria Road, Surbiton, Surrey KT6 4NS
Tel: 01–390 3651/2

A national association, with local branches, for all matters concerning the relief of sufferers from schizophrenia and of their families and dependants. Very helpful publications.

THE OPEN DOOR ASSOCIATION
National Organizer, Mrs M Woodford, 447 Pensby Road, Heswall, Wirral, Merseyside L61 9PQ

Advice and support for those with a morbid fear of going out and travelling on their own (agoraphobia). Local groups. Send s.a.e. for information about booklets, leaflets and cassettes.

THE PATIENTS' ASSOCIATION
Suffolk House, Banbury Road, Oxford OX2 7HN

Represents and furthers the interests of patients and advises individuals. Publishes a list of national self-help groups.

THE PHOBICS SOCIETY
4 Cheltenham Road, Chorlton-cum-Hardy,
Manchester M21 1QN
Tel: 061–881 1937

For promoting the relief and rehabilitation of persons suffering from agoraphobia and other phobic conditions. Local branches.

RELAXATION FOR LIVING
Dunesk, 29 Burwood Park Road,
Walton-on-Thames, Surrey KT12 5LH
Tel: Walton 27826

A registered charity to promote the teaching of physical relaxation to combat the stress, strain, anxiety and tension of modern life. Local groups.

THE SAMARITANS
Headquarters at 17 Uxbridge Road, Slough, Berks SL1 1SN
Tel: Slough 32713/4

A twenty-four-hour telephone counselling service for those in distress and contemplating suicide. Many local branches, with addresses and telephone numbers in local telephone directories.

U and I CLUB
9E Compton Road, London N1 2AP

The name stands for urinary infection in your home and was founded by Mrs Angela Kilmartin to help women with practical advice on the management of chronic cystitis, bladder and vaginal problems.

No longer has membership but publishes two helpful books on cystitis (£2 for both including postage) and provides a private counselling service at £6 per hour.

WEIGHT WATCHERS
635–637 Ajax Avenue, Slough, Berks SL1 4DB
Tel: Slough 70711

An educational service for men, women and children who are 10 or more pounds overweight and who want to lose their excess weight permanently. Weekly classes run through many local groups. Registration fee £1.50 and a weekly fee of £1.50 until you become eligible for Free Lifetime Membership. Advise seeing your doctor first.